Rethinking the New Technology
of Journalism

Rethinking the New Technology of Journalism

How Slowing Down Will Save the News

Seong Jae Min

The Pennsylvania State University Press
University Park, Pennsylvania

Library of Congress Cataloging-in-
Publication Data

Names: Min, Seong-Jae, 1974– author.
Title: Rethinking the new technology of
    journalism : how slowing down will save
    the news / Seong Jae Min.
Description: University Park, Pennsylvania :
    The Pennsylvania State University Press,
    [2022] | Includes bibliographical
    references and index.
Summary: "Explores the role of technology in
    journalism using historical narratives and
    empirical analysis. Argues for slower-paced
    journalism that prioritizes long-term
    collaboration and reflection to enhance
    journalism's core missions and functions
    in society"—Provided by publisher.
Identifiers: LCCN 2021047882 | ISBN
    9780271092485 (hardback) | ISBN
    9780271092492 (paperback)
Subjects: LCSH: Journalism—Technological
    innovations. | Journalism—Social aspects.
Classification: LCC PN4784.T34 M56 2022 |
    DDC 070.4—dc23/eng/20211014
LC record available at https://lccn.loc.gov
    /2021047882

Published by The Pennsylvania State
University Press,
University Park, PA 16802–1003

The Pennsylvania State University Press
is a member of the Association of University
Presses.

It is the policy of The Pennsylvania State
University Press to use acid-free paper.
Publications on uncoated stock satisfy the
minimum requirements of American
National Standard for Information
Sciences—Permanence of Paper for Printed
Library Material, ANSI Z39.48–1992.

Contents

vi

Illustrations

Acknowledgments

From its conception to the final page, many helped make this book possible. I am blessed to have worked together with my wonderful colleagues and students at Pace University who supplied endless inspiration and support. I'd like to specifically thank my colleagues in the communication studies department—Barry Morris, Mary Ann Murphy, Satish Kolluri, Emilie Zaslow, Adam Klein, Marcella Szablewicz, Aditi Paul, Melvin Williams, and Mary Stambaugh. Katherine Fink in Pace's Pleasantville campus also provided valuable input. The students in my "Citizen Journalism and Deliberation" and "Introduction to Journalism" courses over the years shared numerous insights and refreshing ideas, which were incorporated into the present work. Special thanks go to the members of Investigative Reporters & Editors (IRE) whom I surveyed and interviewed in this book. I learned a lot about the workings of real journalistic workplaces from their candid remarks. I'd also like to acknowledge Fr. Eric Zimmer and Dr. Gerald Kosicki, who served as my mentors from my graduate school days. Their guidance and vision helped shape my academic career and the larger contour of this book. My gratitude also goes to the staff at the Pennsylvania State University Press and two anonymous reviewers who provided important editorial support, critique, and encouragement. Ryan Peterson, in particular, oversaw the publication process from the beginning and was tremendously helpful. And, of course, I thank my family who, as always, gave endless love and devotion. Without their assistance and caring support, this book would not have been possible.

Introduction
Journalism and Technology

> We tend to overestimate the effect of a technology in the short run and underestimate the effect in the long run.
>
> —Roy Amara

In the final days of 2012, the *New York Times* published the story "Snow Fall: Avalanche at Tunnel Creek" on its website. It was a landmark event in web journalism. With stunning visuals and interactive features, the documentary-like story by John Branch simulated a deadly avalanche in Washington State's Cascade Mountains that claimed the lives of three skiers. Merging text, photos, animations, maps, and videos, it was ingeniously designed and absolutely pleasing to the eye. The production team consisted of dozens of people, including reporters, graphic designers, videographers, engineers, and even a physicist who re-created an avalanche model.[1] They spent more than six months putting the piece together. The story was a sensation in journalism circles and received both Pulitzer and Peabody awards the following year. It was hailed as a future of journalism.[2]

However, when I asked the students in my "Introduction to Journalism" class to read and enjoy "Snow Fall," I was surprised that their reactions were lukewarm. Granted, it has been some time since the piece was published and the wow factor might have gone in this fast-changing techno-journalism world. Still, the story's compelling narrative and the presentation's creativity and aesthetics were there. When I asked the students why they didn't appreciate it as much as I had expected, there were several answers. First, few of them bothered to read the story. "It was TLDR!" a student said, meaning in internet slang "Too Long, Didn't Read." Many students were overwhelmed by the fifteen-thousand-word opus and got distracted by a variety of different video snippets, sound effects, photos, and interactive graphics that seemed like too many bells and whistles. Other students wondered why the *New York Times* spent so much time and resources for this particular event—an avalanche in the state of Washington. "It is too much. It is like they are showing off that they can do this kind of thing," another student said.

Make no mistake: "Snow Fall" is a good story. It is an exemplary digital work that incorporated a poetic narrative and sensory experiences enabled by multimedia. Not just the artistic presentations but also the research and newsgathering work done by reporters are extensive and meticulous. But let's face it, few people finished reading the story. It is said that a visitor to the story's site spent an average of twelve minutes there.[3] While that is a considerable amount of time by today's web metrics standards, it is hardly enough time to reach even the middle of the story. It was very likely that the visitors just clicked parts of the story instead of actually reading it. And many of them, like my students, must have been entertained by the compelling photos, graphics, and interactive features that took their central focus away. So, after surfing the story randomly, visitors are left with little substance to remember. The technology behind the story must have been impressive to the visitors initially, but soon, they will likely find it obsolete. Besides wowing the visitors for a brief period, it is unclear how much the story actually engaged them so that they could appreciate a good piece of journalism and become more loyal readers of the *Times*.

The case of "Snow Fall" makes us wonder whether this kind of multimedia-rich, technology-driven story is what readers want and what helps them better understand the world. Technology columnist Farhad Manjoo sums up the problem with "Snow Fall," saying it is "an example of excess, a moment when designers indulged their creativity because they now have the technical means to do so, and not because it improved the story or readers' understanding of it."[4] In other words, "Snow Fall" was a story created more for the sake of reporters and storytellers than with the audience experience in mind. It was a story that lacked a careful consideration of audience reception and engagement. With all due respect to its painstaking newsgathering efforts, it was also a story led by technology, not by reporters.

Throughout history, technological innovations have been closely associated with journalistic practices. The invention of the printing press in the fifteenth century allowed the creation of a reading public, which was essential to the growth of journalism; costly and unreliable communication through telegraph in the early nineteenth century sparked journalists to develop the "inverted pyramid" style of writing, in which the most important facts are presented first in a condensed story format. The internet destroyed the advertising-based economy of newsrooms and thus bankrupted traditional newspapers, while contributing to the rise of citizen and alternative journalism backed by digital tools. And the technological affordances of the web platform would allow transformative storytelling experiences like "Snow Fall." As will be illustrated throughout the book, however, these cases are not so simple, such that one cannot make a wholesale, technology-deterministic argument that technology transforms journalism. There are cultural, social, economic, organizational, and political forces at work in the relationship between technology and journalism.

Journalism's pursuit of technology has only accelerated in recent years without much luck. Google Glass was going to reinvent journalism, and many journalism schools created news reporting courses utilizing the product, both of which are now hard to find; robots, or artificial intelligence, are said to be replacing human reporters, though that doesn't seem to be happening in the near future. The decentralized and transparent blockchain is touted to be saving journalism, but it has gained little traction so far. Worse yet, journalism's relentless pursuit of technology these years comes with the pressure of "speed." Granted, the journalism business has always been about speed, breaking stories, and keeping tight deadlines, but journalism's preoccupation with speed has turned into angst and zeal in recent years as the industry saw many newsrooms going bankrupt after failing to adapt to the new media environment. It is now almost imperative for many news organizations to innovate constantly in order to survive in the competitive and fast-changing market. Whether it is chatbots, virtual reality, blockchain, or the next "next big thing," the industry is experimenting with new technologies every day, and with great fervor. Indeed, the only constant in journalism seems to be change. Julie Posetti at the Reuters Institute for the Study of Journalism called this tendency the "Shiny Things Syndrome," referring to newsrooms' obsessive pursuit of technology in the absence of clear, research-informed strategies.[5]

Journalism's relentless pursuit of technological adaptations and innovations begs many questions: How important is technology in journalism? Why do we see this obsession with new and speedy technological innovations? Can journalism be successful without resorting to new technologies? What is the relationship between technological and other innovations in journalism? Ultimately, what is the core identity of journalism? Is it essentially a technology-dominant business? Where does that leave the audience? What about the other principles and missions of journalism?

This book attempts to answer the above questions. To that end, I analyze historical and current cases of journalistic innovations as well as technological narratives around the journalism industry. Surveys of and interviews with editors, reporters, and newsroom technologists will also illuminate how journalism relates to technology. By no means do I argue that technology is an inconsequential factor in journalism. On the contrary, technology has been essential in journalism's survival and progress. My core argument is that while technology is important in journalism, those in journalism circles today believe too much in its power. As they increasingly resort to technological means, hoping that new tools and inventions will rescue journalism from its current crisis, they ignore why journalism exists in the first place. Swept by the technologically deterministic narrative, they forget the field's civic and democratic missions.

And they are going too fast without a clear aim and research, often threatened by the power of such technology giants as Google and Facebook. I argue that viable journalistic advancement through technology takes careful research, trial and error, and, most of all, significant time and ripened social settings. Viewed this way, technology's impact on journalism is not necessarily immediate and sweeping; its true impact is shaped over time and is also affected by various social, cultural, economic, political, and organizational factors.

Toward the end of the book, I situate my critical analysis within the broader framework of "slow journalism." Slow journalism, born out of the larger slow movement—along with slow living, slow foods, and environmentally conscious consumption—refers to the idea that good journalism is not bound by time pressure and is more mindful and sustainable.[6] The slow journalism movement so far has focused mostly on slow and insightful news reporting and consumption. I expand the idea of slow journalism to include journalism's attitudes toward technological innovations. The slow journalism movement can provide some antidote to the journalism industry's unrelenting pursuit of speedy technological adaptations that may come at the expense of good reporting. Ultimately, it makes us think over what journalism means in today's ever-changing technological environment.

Between Technological Determinism and Social Construction of Technology

A logical opening idea on the topic of technology's impact on journalism is surveying the two principal theories that are popular in science and technology studies (STS): technological determinism and social construction (or shaping) of technology. These theories have a long history and are well enough established to inform the roles of technology in journalism. Before discussing specific cases of technologies in the following chapters, I overview these theories as a guiding framework.

First, the often controversial yet dominant technological determinism suggests that the development of technology proceeds in an autonomous manner, determined by an internal logic independent of social influence, and that technological change drives social change in a prescribed fashion.[7] It is a straightforward and attractive idea. After all, when social media connects you with people anytime, anywhere, when 3D-printers churn out almost any physical object, when artificial intelligence writes on your behalf, and when your car is driving by itself, it is difficult to shake the feeling that technologies are changing the world and humans are just tagging along. Indeed, technological determinism is very popular in the business world, where cutthroat competitions for innovations and productivity exist; in popular culture where the power of machine is mythicized in novels, movies, and television shows; and in the intersection of academia and popular culture, where the Canadian media theorist Marshall McLuhan's idea that "the medium is the message"—meaning that the communication technologies humans created have become a central nervous system that may alter the ways humans experience the world—has gained a massive following.[8]

Historians and scholars of technology produced many compelling accounts that affirm the determining power of modern technologies. For example, the invention of the gun changed how combat was waged and determined the winner and loser in warfare—and, eventually, the survival of a civilization. After all, what could the swords, bows, and arrows of Native Americans do against European colonizers' guns firing fast from a safe distance? Other fascinating examples include how the invention of the telegraph revolutionized business communication, by providing instantaneous message transmission, and also expanded police and fire services, which used it as an alarm system in major cities of the United States in the nineteenth century.[9] In the business world, historian Alfred Chandler's *The Visible Hand*—in which he made a case that modern managerial capitalism was the product of the technological revolution of modern times—still stands as a revered work.[10]

At the other end of the spectrum, however, resides the theory known as the social construction of technology. Its supporters, also known as social constructivists, espouse the idea of the social shaping of technology, believing that how technology is embedded in social contexts is essential to understanding the power and effects of the technology.[11] It is the idea that the agency, values, and norms of humans are more important than the technology itself.

As Raymond Williams said, "Technological determinism is an untenable notion because it substitutes for real social, political, and economic intention, either the random autonomy of invention or an abstract human essence."[12] Williams famously argued that an interlock of military, political, and commercial intentions, as well as democratic interests, is at play in the design and use of science and technology. Consider the case of guns, above used as an example of technological determinism. It is easy to imagine that the Native Americans succumbed helplessly to the guns of the early colonizers. But one can argue that it was more of an epidemic widespread at the time—and that their leaders' failed tactics and psychological gaffes, rather than the guns, defeated them, because their longbow technology was not necessarily inferior to the colonizers' guns of the time, which were limited by recoil and slow rates of firing. It is inconceivable that an army of eighty thousand Native Americans was instantly defeated solely by the guns of fewer than two hundred Spanish soldiers, as illustrated vividly in Jared Diamond's masterwork, *Guns, Germs, and Steel*.[13] And if one looks at how guns are employed across the world today, different human cultures and values determine their usage and effects, giving the idea that society and culture shape the gun technology. Indeed, historians who have looked closely at the relationship between technology and society tend to support the proposition that technologies are not autonomous but are social products, susceptible to social and democratic controls.[14] Scholars have shown that, for example, so-called urban technologies such as telephones, radio, and automobiles have been used differently by rural populations, creating individual versions of "rural modernity."[15] In another well-known example, it is argued that the evolution of the design of bicycles has been nonlinear, shaped by the needs and concerns of both users and nonusers in various stages.[16]

The seemingly conflicting theories of technological determinism and social construction of technology are not necessarily irreconcilable. First, between the "hard" technological determinists (who believe that technologies develop independently from societal concerns) and the "radical" or postmodern social constructivists (who believe that even the truth and nature of scientific knowledge and technical workings of machines themselves are constructed by social processes) there exist moderates who would focus on the degree, scope, and context of technology development and use in society. They would ask such questions as to what extent, in what ways, and under what scope and conditions particular groups of people are able to shape their sociotechnical systems. Phrased differently, the questions are to what extent, in what ways, and under what conditions particular kinds of technology are more autonomous and powerful in shaping society.[17] So, the task here is to acknowledge the mutual and interconnected influence of both technology and human agency and probe specific contexts where particular factors may be more influential.

Some scholars provide useful insights to reconcile the two theories. For example, the American computer scientist and futurist Roy Amara once said that people "tend to overestimate the effect of a technology in the short run and underestimate the effect in the long run."[18] This adage is now often dubbed Amara's Law. The point of this clever remark is the importance of time in technology development and adoption. When an invention or discovery appears, people tend to get hyped or overly concerned about the possibilities it may bring: Behold! The cars will drive by themselves, robots will replace the human workforce, and so on. The stocks of the companies associated with the technologies become overheated. But as time goes by, people usually get to observe many failures and, if any, a limited and slow development and adoption of the technology, however promising it was in the beginning. At this point of the technology development cycle, critics also chime in and warn about the hype associated with it. So, people get disappointed and forget about it, but at some point, the technology becomes ubiquitous and tremendously changes their lives. Such were the cases of electricity, steam engines, and computers. All these technologies came with short-term hype, followed by skepticism and, eventually, a fundamental impact on human life that we today regard as ubiquitous and natural. In 1998, against the hype that the internet would bring a new transformative information economy, the Nobel Prize–winning economist Paul Krugman claimed, "By 2005 or so, it will become clear that the Internet's impact on the economy has been no greater than the fax machine's."[19] Predicting the future is a notoriously difficult task, even for a Nobel Prize winner, but this quote today sounds just comical.

As will be illustrated in more detail in the next chapter, many technologies—both historical and modern—followed Amara's Law. Highly touted contemporary technologies in journalism, such as virtual reality and artificial intelligence, started as early as the mid-twentieth century and their advancement has been slow and painful. What Amara's Law suggests is that the adoption and development of technologies take time and they go through cycles of hype and disappointment until some of them become more available for use by the general public, which resonates with the findings of some popular academic studies in business and communication.[20] In particular, Amara's Law is well illustrated in the "hype cycles," developed by the

American information technology and business consulting firm Gartner, which suggests that new technologies and innovations go through five stages of adoption: (1) innovation trigger, (2) peak of inflated expectations, (3) trough of disillusionment, (4) slope of enlightenment, and (5) plateau of productivity.

From the perspective of Amara's Law, the theories of technological determinism and social construction of technology may sound not so antithetical. That is, in the longer term, technologies may indeed have a determining impact on human life but, in the shorter term, human agency has more power in shaping and constructing the technologies. Technology historian Thomas Misa supports this point when he observes that technologically deterministic scholarship tends to adopt a macro perspective, looking at larger scales of time and space, whereas social constructivist scholarship tends to adopt a micro perspective, looking at the details of human-technology interactions in relatively smaller scales of time and space.[21] According to Misa, philosophers of technology who utilize abstraction and macro-level thinking tend to adopt technologically deterministic thinking. They develop grand theories of society and technological changes, as seen in Jacques Ellul's work on technology as a complete social system.[22] However, Misa argues that the idea of machines as a powerful causal force bringing change vanishes when historians adopt a more detailed analysis. For many business and labor historians who adopt micro-level analysis, technology is a subject of negotiation reflecting human agency. "Again and again, historians writing large-scale or deterministic accounts deploy the Machine to structure social change, while as soon as the historical microscope is unveiled, the Machine as such dissolves," writes Misa.[23]

The attempt to reconcile technological determinism and the social construction of technology can also be found in well-known organizational behavior literature. Gerardine DeSanctis and Marshall Scott Poole, who studied the role of information technologies in organizational changes, supply a middle-of-the-road perspective about the power of technology.[24] Their "adaptive structuration" theory suggests that structures in technology and structures in human action are continually intertwined, shaping each other. This perspective is a departure from the decision-making school in organizational behavior that emphasizes technology as a deterministic force that brings productivity and efficiency to organizations;[25] it is also a departure from the institutional school that argues people generate social constructions of technology using resources, interpretive schemes, and norms embedded in the larger institutional context.[26] DeSanctis and Poole argue that there is a "dialectic of control" between the group and the technology. That is, technology structures shape the group, but the group likewise shapes its own interaction, exerting control over the use of technology structures and the new structures that emerge from their use. Organizational change occurs gradually, as technology structures are appropriated and begin to change decision processes. Over time, new social structures may become a part of larger organizational life. In this way, technologies can serve to trigger organizational change, although they cannot fully determine it, DeSanctis and Poole propose. Their theory is quite useful as it illustrates that the integration of technologies into journalism is not a simple plug-in process but a complex socio-organizational process. This theory is further utilized in later chapters.

Although the literature introduced above attempts to find a middle way between technological determinism and social construction of technology, it appears that more weight is given to the idea of human agency shaping the technology, at least in the short term. Such a tendency is apparent from Misa, who says that "from a shop-floor perspective, the Machine is an irrelevant abstraction, and what makes history is individuals (perhaps classes) in conflict or accommodation."[27] Although not explicit, DeSanctis and Poole, who developed their theory based on the renowned British sociologist Anthony Giddens's grand idea of structuration, also seem to emphasize human agency. Gidden's "structuration" refers to the production and reproduction of the social systems through members' use of rules and resources in interaction.[28] Here, "interaction" signals the idea that humans have a say against the larger social structures. In DeSanctis and Poole's adaptive structuration, they further develop the idea of human agency: human beings exercise *conscious* choices to intentionally adopt rules and resources to accomplish organizational goals.

A similar observation can be made in terms of journalistic innovation. The dominant discourse, especially within the journalism industry, has been that of technological determinism. Journalists and industry insiders tend to regard technology and technological development as an inevitable force that directly causes changes in journalism, as shown in a slew of academic research as well as in chapter 2 of this book.[29] In the early days of the internet revolution, journalism academics also took a decidedly technologically deterministic stance, as did many media scholars.[30] But later work dealing with journalism and technology favors more nuanced and balanced explanations, placing technology in specific organizational, cultural, political, and economic contexts.[31] For example, Will Mari's study of newsroom computerization shows a mutual shaping of technology and human agency such that certain computer technologies give rise to certain affordances compatible with newsroom norms and culture, which influences journalists' sense of control and engagement with those technologies.[32]

In general, the journalism industry, the larger business circles, and the popular narrative tend to believe in technological determinism. But academics of STS and journalism studies increasingly subscribe to the tenets of social construction of technology. In fact, recent scholarship appears to have discarded the notion of simple technological determinism. This does not necessarily mean that the perspective of social construction of technology is superior to technological determinism. However, beyond the popular and grand narrative of technological determinism in history, and beyond the dominant business perspective that adopts a more technologically deterministic way of thinking, there is a need to analyze more nuanced details of technology-human interactions. As Pablo Boczkowski showed in his study of newsroom technology, this approach does not replace but complements a concern with the effects of technologies on journalism—precisely because the technological effects are potentially so significant that we need to have a better understanding of the processes that generate them.[33] And that's exactly what I plan to achieve by looking at the history of the technological impact on journalism.

Chapter 1 probes technology's impact on journalism in detail, from the printing press to blockchain. A microscopic analysis of historical as well as current technology adoption suggests that journalism's innovations are often determined by sociocultural contexts, rather than by technologies themselves, and that their adoption process is slow and gradual. Chapter 2 investigates why there is so much push for technological innovations in journalism. Utilizing the French sociologist Pierre Bourdieu's field theory as a general theoretical framework, it argues that the professional journalistic field, which is rapidly losing its jurisdictional control, attempts to reassert its boundaries using technological means. This chapter also includes some empirical materials, such as surveys of journalists' roles and attitudes in their workplace, and an analysis of technology discourse in journalism trade publications, showing that journalists today live by the grand discourse of technology, struggling to keep up with the new tools and innovations. In chapter 3, I introduce the slow movement and apply its tenets to journalism and technological innovation, arguing that slow values make journalistic innovations more sustainable. Analyzing the cases of *USA Today*, the *Guardian*, and *Buzz-Feed*, I then show how journalistic innovation can come from many different dimensions beyond technology, which include people, culture, and norms. In the conclusion, I advance the thesis of the book by arguing that the industry's heavy focus on speedy technological innovation has marginalized journalism's civic missions and democratic concerns. Overall, this book urges those involved in journalism to think beyond the dominant technology narrative.

From the Printing Press to Blockchain

The Social Shaping of Journalism
Technologies

> Computers are useless. They can only give you answers.
>
> —Pablo Picasso

Journalism's kinship with technology is not a recent phenomenon. It is conventional wisdom that media and communication technologies transform the way we communicate, including how news is produced and consumed. Many journalism practitioners and media scholars tend to endorse this view that technologies are determining forces of news production and dissemination.[1] For example, Brian McNair once declared, "The form and content of journalism is crucially determined by the available technology of newsgathering, production, and dissemination."[2] It is true that technology does impact newsgathering and distribution processes, but a dominant focus on the power of technological form may hamper our understanding of how technologies interact with surrounding sociocultural contexts.

While technologies are a powerful force, they rarely bring changes by themselves. The impact of technologies on journalism may not be the same across news organizations, economies, and countries. The impact may also take a long time to be felt, gradually mediated by various social and organizational factors. Patricia Dooley, who looked at the long history of journalism technologies, thus concludes that "news is so strongly related to factors such as writers, readers, and external variables such as social and cultural values, intellectual traditions, and economics that it is simply impossible for it to change for only one reason."[3]

To further substantiate my claims, I discuss how technologies that are closely associated with journalistic innovations are often shaped by social situations. I focus on the following technologies: the printing press, the telegraph, computers and the internet, virtual and augmented reality technologies, artificial intelligence, and blockchain. These are widely regarded as the technologies that have transformed or will transform journalism.[4] Numerous smaller-scale technologies in journalism have existed, but they were short-lived and mostly succumbed to economic reality.[5] If it can be demonstrated that such monumental technologies as the printing press were also, to a degree, subject to social circumstances, the argument that technology is not an uncontrollable, autonomous force will likely be strengthened and our understanding of the interaction between technology and society will be expanded.

The Printing Press and the Birth of Newspapers

The printing press is one of the most important inventions in history and left no field of human enterprise untouched (see fig. 1). Scholars and historians provide fascinating accounts of how the invention by the German printer Johannes Gutenberg around 1440 led to a rise in literacy among the general public and awakened their individuality, which challenged religious authority and ultimately led to the Reformation, the Renaissance, and the birth of modern nation-states.[6] Historian Elizabeth Eisenstein, in one of the more complete accounts of the impact of the printing press, concludes by saying, "The communications shift altered the way Western Christians viewed their sacred book and the natural world. It made the words of God appear more multiform and His handiwork more uniform. The printing press laid the basis for both literal fundamentalism and for modern science. It remains indispensable for humanistic scholarship. It is still responsible for our museum-without-walls."[7]

In journalism history, too, the printing press is probably the most important invention, in that it gave birth to modern newspapers. The change from hand-copied to printed news was a milestone event in journalism history, as the mass circulation of news gave regular publicity to the events and personalities of political life across Europe.[8] Around 1605, the first publication that could be called a newspaper appeared in Strasbourg—then part of Germany and a town not far from Mainz, where Gutenberg lived and worked his whole life (see fig. 2).[9] Soon, widespread distribution of newspapers began across

Figure 1 Gutenberg press, reproduction. Photo: Flickr / Andrew Plumb (CC-BY-SA 2.0).

Europe throughout the seventeenth century and a little later in North America.[10]

It would not be wrong to say that newspapers began their existence thanks to the printing press. After all, how can you mass produce and distribute news on paper without the printing press? But a wholesale cause-effect claim that the technology of the printing press created newspapers ignores the historical, cultural, and social contexts surrounding the technology and fails to answer why and how newspapers became widespread. Here I introduce some major counterpoints that show the importance of social and cultural structures in the development of the printing press and newspapers.

Figure 2 Title page of *Relation*, the world's first newspaper, 1609. University Library of Heidelberg. Photo: Wikimedia Commons / University Library of Heidelberg.

First, the fact that the impact of the printing press felt much less noticeable in East Asia, and that the development of newspapers there was rather slow, suggests that sociocultural forces were at work in the adoption and use of the technology as well as newspapers. It is by now an accepted historical fact that the printing press technology began in East Asia, way before Gutenberg. Woodblock printing started in China before the eighth century, and the Chinese alchemist Bi Sheng experimented with a movable type in the eleventh century. The Chinese technology spread to neighboring countries, and in 1234 the first books known to have been printed in a metallic typeset were published in Korea, where printing reached its highest development.[11] Therefore, celebrating Gutenberg as the inventor of the printing press represents a Eurocentric historical perspective, although his machine was quite a developed one. However, it is true that the printing press, books, and newspapers became much more widely and quickly spread and their impact felt stronger in Europe than in East Asia. So what accounts for the differences? A common explanation is the complexity of East Asian languages, requiring several types for each character, which reduced the practicability of movable type printing in China, Korea, and Japan.[12]

Beyond the complexity of Asian languages, there is perhaps a more convincing explanation about the slow spread of the printing press and newspapers in East Asia: the social-cultural-economic differences between the East and the West at the time. That is, emerging capitalism and the rise of a literate middle class in Western Europe combined with the printing press technology after the fifteenth century to produce the information revolution and a massive impact on society, which wasn't the case in East Asia. In Western Europe, the enterprising spirit of capitalism played a key role. The early printers were urban entrepreneurs who pioneered publishing for profit and they also served as "literary dispensers of glory," taking pride in serving humanity at large with new knowledge.[13] Then, the increasingly powerful middle class and their rising literacy led to an increased demand for books and newspapers. The European middle class was willing to pay for works of writing, creating an even larger demand and further development in the printing technology. But in the East, such a dynamic did not exist. There, reading had been historically reserved mostly for nobles, Confucian scholars, and Buddhist monks. Despite the availabilities of printing technologies, the strong central government of East Asia strictly controlled publications. It is believed that newspapers in China emerged as early as in the mid-Tang dynasty (618–907), but they were mainly official publications circulated among bureaucrats and scholar-officials. They were issued and managed by the central administration of the government, a tradition still alive in China today.[14] China's publication of books and newspapers, furthermore, was also without capitalistic motivations because printing facilitated the continuity and universality of the written language, and thus became an important vehicle for sustaining cultural tradition, as is evident in the printing of the Confucian classics and similar material for civil service examinations.[15] A similar trend can be found in Korea, which experienced numerous foreign invasions and loss of precious cultural items. For the central Korean government at the time, preserving cultural artifacts was a top concern. Therefore, Koreans invented and used the metal movable type to preserve and maintain the most complete and comprehensive Buddhist scripts in the world, *Tripitaka Koreana*. In other words, the main motivation for using the printing press in Korea was not the mass distribution of writings but the preservation of cultural artifacts. As this case illustrates, the socioeconomic and cultural differences between the two societies influenced the development of the printing press and newspapers.

Second, even in Europe, where the impact of the printing press felt monumental and ubiquitous, there is evidence that the development of technology and of newspapers had been slow and conditioned by numerous factors. The French historians Lucien Febvre and Henri-Jean Martin suggest that the impact of the printing press and books was monumental for Europe, but their development was a gradual process, just one element of larger transformations at the time—it was evolutionary, not revolutionary. National policies, geographic locations, and economic and social aspects factored into the evolution of the printing press and book publication.[16] The invention was also gradual in that, before Gutenberg, there were inventors like Laurens Coster of the Netherlands and Panfilo Castaldi of Italy.[17] Gutenberg's machine was an aggregation and adaptation of technologies that had been used for a long time, such as olive presses and woodblock print type.[18] Perhaps it would be more accurate to say that Gutenberg "perfected" the technology by treating typesetting and printing as two separate steps.

More importantly, the impact of the printing press on newspapers was beginning to be felt at least a full century after the invention. The first newspapers—rather than irregular broadsides or pamphlets—only began to emerge in the early seventeenth century, more than 150 years after Gutenberg's printing press. Historian Andrew Pettegree explains that this was because the printers followed a very conservative strategy, concentrating on the publication of books most familiar to the medieval manuscript tradition.[19] Instead, for much of the sixteenth century, news was distributed mostly through handwritten manuscripts, especially for the elite. Furthermore, unlike the more salacious content found in pamphlets, emerging newspapers carried dry, official, and complex accounts and thus struggled for at least a hundred years to find a place in the market. Pettegree concludes his work by emphasizing the importance of social norms in newspaper production and distribution: "The arrival of print in the mid-fifteenth century offered many new opportunities; but it had to make its way in a world where networks for the distribution of news had already been developed: networks with standards, conventions and social freight with which those in circles of power were fully conversant. In the centuries that followed, print disrupted and then reshaped this infrastructure, bringing new customers into the circle of news but without fully superseding the established norms."[20]

As such, newspaper development in Europe was a gradual social process. Newspapers evolved in stages such that, in the beginning, occasional broadsides and news sheets emerged that were subject to government censorship and licensing requirements, but as both the freedom of the press and the market for the reading public expanded, more regular and independent newspapers appeared.

The point can also be illustrated if we move to the American continent and look at its early newspapers. The printing press first came to Cambridge, Massachusetts, in British North America in 1638 and played a significant role in providing religious materials to the colonists. America's first printing shop, owned by a reverend, printed a broadside, the *Freeman's Oath*, and the famous *Bay Psalm Book* for the religious edification of the colonists.[21] Beyond a series of broadsides and pamphlets, America saw its first multipage newspaper, *Publick Occurrences Both Forreign and Domestick*, published in Boston in 1690. This historic paper's fate was doomed after just a single issue because the powerful colonial British government shut it down immediately, saying it was printed without permission. Exactly why the government censored the newspaper is under dispute, but it is most likely that it contained content criticizing the British government and royal families in Europe.[22] Now compare the fate of *Publick Occurrences* to that of the *New York Weekly Journal* about half a century later. In 1733, the New York newspaper published articles criticizing the British royal governor of that period, William Cosby. Cosby condemned the newspaper and tried to close it down. But this time, the case was sent to the New York Supreme Court, where high-profile lawyers successfully defended John Zenger, the publisher of the paper. The Zenger trial of 1735 was a landmark case in the history of American journalism, in which the press was given the right to criticize the government, which laid the groundwork for the United States' important First Amendment principle in 1789—the freedom of the press.

Both *Publick Occurrences* and the *New York Weekly Journal* engaged in similar criticism of the government. So, what made one successful and not the other? In 1690, when *Publick Occurrences* was published, the British royal government's social control was stronger. Furthermore, Massachusetts's Supreme Court was established only in 1692 and the proper legal system was just not there. But in 1734–35, when the Zenger trial was underway, British control of North America had become weaker. The New York Supreme Court, America's oldest supreme court, was established in 1691, and, over time, it had established a unique pattern for American adjudication, stronger than that found in other colonial states, such as Massachusetts.[23] Although not without scandals, the growing independence and professionalization of the New York bar must have played out favorably for Zenger. It is likely that the fate of *Publick Occurrences* and the *New York Weekly Journal* diverged because of the differences in the legal structures and historical atmospheres in which the two papers were printed. In other words, one can make an argument that it was the social system that decided the life and death of America's first newspapers.

The Telegraph and the Inverted Pyramid Style of Writing

The invention of the telegraph in the early to mid-nineteenth century was another landmark event in the history of communication technologies. The technology was in development throughout the eighteenth and early nineteenth centuries by many inventors and researchers, but it was the American inventor Samuel Morse who popularized the telegraph with his Morse code (fig. 3). In 1844, Morse sent his first telegraph message from Washington, DC, to Baltimore, and by 1853, almost all states in the United States were

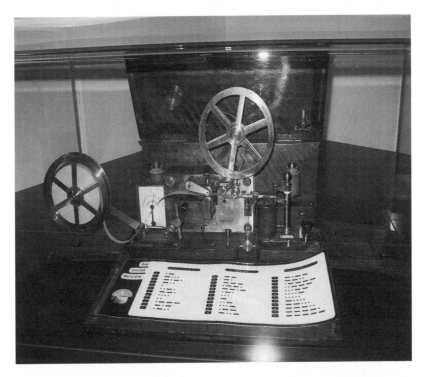

Figure 3 Morse telegraph, 1837. Historical collection of France Telecom. Photo: Wikimedia Commons / Zubro (CC-BY-SA).

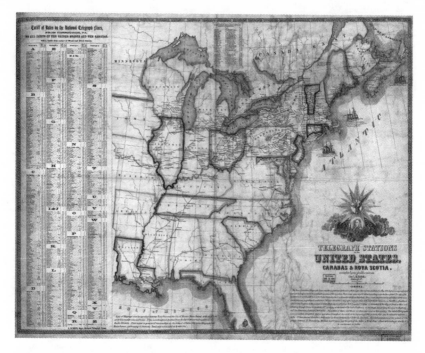

Figure 4 Map of telegraph stations in the United States, 1853. Library of Congress, Geography and Map Division, Samuel F. Morse Papers Collection, G3701.P92 1853 .B2 TIL.

connected by the technology (fig. 4). By 1866, a transatlantic telegraph line had been laid, connecting America and Europe. The lightning-fast long-distance communication enabled by the telegraph revolutionized many domains of society, changing the way people conducted business, politics, and war.

Journalism, the business of handling information, was of course affected by this revolutionary technology. The practice of newsgathering and dissemination became quicker and more efficient. New patterns of news communication had emerged. The technology changed people's sense of space and time and thus changed how people thought about communication itself, as James Carey has suggested.[24] One particularly important change, which most journalism textbooks mention, was the introduction of the so-called inverted pyramid style of writing, in which the most important facts are summarized in the beginning and less crucial details are placed toward the end of a story. Since then, the inverted pyramid style has become the gold standard of modern news writing, typifying the ideals of objectivity, neutrality, and efficiency. The conventional wisdom is that the early telegraph, which was costly and often unreliable, forced reporters to summarize the key facts in the beginning.[25] Eminent communication scholar Everett Rogers writes, "The telegraph affected American journalism in yet other ways. For example, AP correspondents were instructed to put the most important facts in the first sentence of each news story, with less crucial information in each succeeding sentence. The 'inverted pyramid' style of news writing was necessary because telegraphic services from the Civil War battlefields were occasionally disrupted, and it was essential for the highest-priority information to get through to newspapers using the AP service."[26]

Indeed, the widely accepted view is that the telegraph technology during the American Civil War (1861–65) gave birth to the inverted pyramid style of writing. This view sounds logical and convincing. The early telegraph was not a reliable technology and it was also expensive. Reporters in the war zones had to send breaking news via telegraph and they put the most important message in the very beginning for fear of losing communication midway, the explanation goes. But if one analyzes this history with a microscope, the technological deterministic explanation gets shattered. A handful of empirical content analysis suggests that it was long after the invention of the telegraph that the inverted pyramid style of writing became popularized in newspapers. A survey of representative American newspapers between 1860 and 1910 found that it was not until 1895 that even 1 percent of all stories analyzed had the inverted pyramid style; it was only after the 1900s that a significant number of stories were written in such a manner.[27] Another content analysis of the *New York Times* and the *New York Herald* in a similar time frame found that only between 1875 and 1895 did the share of inverted pyramid news stories rapidly increase to about a quarter.[28] Yet another comprehensive content analysis of American daily newspapers between 1865 and 1954 found that inverted pyramids were rarely used until the 1880s.[29] The available evidence points toward the fact that the inverted pyramid style began as late as the 1900s or as early as around 1875–80. This time frame is much later than the invention of the telegraph in 1844 and its US-wide adoption around the 1850s. It is also at least a decade after the end of the Civil War in 1865.

The AP's breaking news coverage of President Lincoln's assassination on April 14, 1865, is illustrative. If AP reporters had been really instructed to write their stories in the inverted pyramid style, then we would have certainly seen a summary-style lead in the coverage of such a monumental event as Lincoln's death. Instead, we got this:

WASHINGTON, APRIL 14—President Lincoln and wife visited Ford's Theatre this evening for the purpose of witnessing the performance of "The American Cousin." It was announced in the papers that Gen. Grant would also be present, but that gentleman took the late train of cars for New Jersey.

The theatre was densely crowded, and everybody seemed delighted with the scene before them. During the third act and while there was a temporary pause for one of the actors to enter, a sharp report of a pistol was heard, which merely attracted attention, but suggested nothing serious until a man rushed to the front of the President's box, waving a long dagger in his right hand, exclaiming, "Sic semper tyrannis," and immediately leaped from the box, which was in the second tier, to the stage beneath, and ran across to the opposite side, made his escape amid the bewilderment of the audience from the rear of the theatre, and mounted a horse and fled.

The groans of Mrs. Lincoln first disclosed the fact that the President had been shot, when all present rose to their feet rushing toward the stage, many exclaiming, "Hang him, hang him!" The excitement was of the wildest possible description. . . .

There was a rush towards the President's box, when cries were heard—"Stand back and give him air!" "Has anyone stimulants?" On a hasty examination it was found that the President had been shot through the head above and back of the temporal bone, and that some of his brain was oozing out. He was removed to a private house opposite the theatre, and the Surgeon General of the Army and other surgeons were sent for to attend to his condition.

On an examination of the private box, blood was discovered on the back of the cushioned rocking chair on which the President had been sitting; also on the partition and on the floor. A common single-barreled pocket pistol was found on the carpet.

A military guard was placed in front of the private residence to which the President had been conveyed. An immense crowd was in front of it, all deeply anxious to learn the condition of the President.

It had been previously announced that the wound was mortal, but all hoped otherwise. . . .

At midnight the Cabinet, with Messrs. Sumner, Colfax and Farnsworth, Judge Curtis, Governor Oglesby, Gen. Meigs, Col. Hay, and a few personal friends, with Surgeon General Barnes and his immediate assistants, were around his bedside.

The President was in a state of syncope, totally insensible and breathing slowly. The blood oozed from the wound at the back of his head. The surgeons exhausted every effort of medical skill, but all hope was gone.[30]

It is only in the middle of the story that the readers realize the president was shot, and they are informed that he is dead in the very last paragraph. Are there more newsworthy items than a popular president getting shot in the head? Shouldn't it have been the logical case that such a significant event be written with a summary lead, informing readers what happened right away? The fact that the AP's seasoned White House correspondent Lawrence Gobright wrote the event up in this way suggests that the inverted pyramid style was not the norm of writing at the time.

Certainly, the telegraph or the wire service is not the direct cause of the inverted pyramid style of writing. So, what made reporters in the late nineteenth and early twentieth century adopt the practice? A couple of plausible explanations do exist. Marcus Errico and colleagues, who did a thorough content analysis, suggest that the inverted pyramid style came about during the Progressive Era in the United States (ca. 1880–1910). They argue that it was the era's surge in scientific thinking and its revolution in education that had brought the inverted pyramids: the young reporters of the Progressive Era saw themselves as social scientists and political reformers who sought solutions to society's problems through the application of wit. As these reporters took up the journalistic workplace, they began to produce objective, fact-based writing, of which the inverted pyramid style was a part.[31] Another convincing explanation comes from Horst Pöttker, who focused on communicative and economic reasons: inverted pyramids and other associated writing changes—such as the reduction of sentence length, the illustration of articles with drawings and photographs, the use of headlines, and the sorting of news into specific sections—took place in the late nineteenth century to enhance the communicative quality of the journalistic product, which was meant to appeal to mass audiences more effectively. This aim to reach a larger readership and create publicness is also connected with the economic considerations of American publishers eager to enhance the usefulness of their papers.[32] Yet from another perspective, David Mindich argues that the inverted pyramids originated from the Civil War and the murder of Lincoln.

According to Mindich, Edwin M. Stanton, secretary of war for the Union during the Civil War, who was unpopular but power-hungry, favored the pyramid when preparing official bulletins because the form and objective, factual style were better suited to sway public opinion in the interests of the government.[33] Mindich's explanation emphasizes political factors in the development of inverted pyramids. It is convincing but at odds with the content analysis findings discussed earlier—that the inverted pyramid form began sometime between the 1880s and the 1900s. Still, Mindich's explanation points toward the importance of sociopolitical factors in the rise of the inverted pyramid form.

It is difficult to pinpoint the direct cause of the inverted pyramid form. It could be for political, economic, communicative, or historical reasons— and probably was some combination of all of them. What is clear is that the technological explanation, that the costly and unreliable telegraph is responsible for the rise of the inverted pyramid form, is less convincing. The available evidence gives more weight to the idea that the inverted pyramid style of writing is an invention born out of the specific historical and sociocultural contexts of the United States. Had the technology indeed been the direct cause of the inverted pyramid form, we would have seen at least some similar styles of writing in mid- to late nineteenth-century newspapers in Western Europe, where the telegraph was widely used. But no such evidence exists, and the European tradition of literary and often partisan journalism seemed unaffected at the time and has remained strong for much of the twentieth century.[34] The inverted pyramid is a unique product originating in the market-oriented American media system at a specific point of history.

The Long and Winding Road to Newsroom Computerization

The image of a journalist using a typewriter, probably with a cigar in the corner of the mouth and the occasional beating of the jammed keys, is long gone. Such an image is romantic and stereotyped. Today's journalists are equipped with the latest computer tools and move fast and relentlessly to conduct their business. Computers have become essential tools of the journalistic craft and it is inconceivable now to imagine journalism without them. But it is not as though computers suddenly replaced every typewriter and piece of paper and transformed every newsroom overnight. As Amara's Law suggests, they followed cycles of hypes and bubbles, until they became so ubiquitous that we find them to be a natural part of the industry. The process of computerization is also marked with conflicts and struggles in the newsroom. In so doing, not only the technology but also human agency shaped the direction of journalism. This section looks at the brief history of newsroom computerization, pre-internet.

The computerization of American newsrooms began quite long ago. Giant computers—mainframes—were adopted by some news organizations as early as the 1950s, although they were used mostly for human resources and business administration purposes. Will Mari's work well illustrates the stages of newsroom computerization before the internet: the mainframe era from the mid-1950s to the 1960s, the minicomputer era between the 1970s and the early 1980s, and the microprocessor era of powerful personal computers up until around 1992, just before the internet revolution began.[35]

Many things happened during these thirty to forty years of computerization between the mid-1950s and the early 1990s, and the process was convoluted. In the beginning, mainframes were used only by a few wealthy news publishers, because they were too big and expensive. Before the ubiquitous desktop computers and word processing software in the early 1990s, journalists used the clunky and often unreliable optical character recognition (OCR) scanning technology to electronically prepare their texts and, a little bit later, video display terminals (VDTs), the precursors of personal computers. For the news distribution side, there was the once-popular videotex technology, a system that utilized telephone lines to display text on the audience's televisions. These technologies started with outsized expectations and hype, evolved fast with many variations, and died rather quickly.[36] Then, journalistic work on powerful personal computers with word processing began. However, even when it came to writing with reliable word processors on desktop computers, the process has not always been smooth for many writers. Although not specifically focused on journalists, Matthew Kirschenbaum, in his literary history of word processing, described how "the story of writing in the digital age is every bit as messy as the ink-stained rags that would have littered the floor of Gutenberg's print shop or the hot molten lead of the Linotype machine," suggesting that writers on word processors experienced a litany of fears, hopes, struggles, and confrontations.[37] It is not as though those powerful computers just showed up one day and journalists had a rude awakening—journalists weren't just tagging along with the technology, feeling helpless. As Mari explains, "It takes something like 30 years to get a handle on what, exactly, a new means of news delivery means for paying the bills. Newsroom computerization is no exception, and was a long and messy process."[38]

Some notable points in newsroom computerization history show the influence of human agency. First, the initial adoption of computers in the 1960s was driven by human needs and institutional-commercial dynamics. The journalists of the time—mostly newspaper and wire reporters—were seeking a means to process the ever-increasing amount of information they handled, which made them more receptive to the idea of computers in the newsroom. This need grew further thanks to the American Newspaper Publishers Association (ANPA), then a powerful industry group, which was concerned about the power of television broadcasting news as well as the rising newspaper production cost. The ANPA thus actively sought computerization as a means of fighting off rivals and saving costs. In collaboration with the Massachusetts Institute of Technology, the ANPA established a research institute studying computerization, and this was one of the reasons that the newspaper industry was among the first in the United States to adopt and integrate computers into their daily work routines.[39] The ANPA also held annual technical conferences, which brought together newspaper people and technology vendors. Wilson Locke, who led the computerization efforts of the *Los Angeles Times*, suggested that these conferences helped form the confederacy between news workers and vendors, which was instrumental in the newspaper's computerization project. Locke further documented that the *Los Angeles Times* embarked on one of the earliest and largest computerization processes in 1974, an arduous seven-year odyssey. As he explained:

> Building the system was slow and complicated. . . . Then we were plagued with a rash of delays. The typesetting program was not working, and an expert was hired to resolve the problems. Next, a glitch developed in interfacing the terminals. Every time one fire was put out, another would start. In the latter part of the sixth year, amid feelings of despair and desperation, it was no longer funny when someone asked when they would have a system. The publisher, managers, and editorial staff were losing confidence and interest in the project. Then, by mutual agreement, the project was abandoned because of the delays and mounting costs.[40]

But a more effective and reliable second generation of systems had arrived, and with accumulated knowledge and experience, the *Los Angeles Times* was able to resume its efforts and successfully incorporate the computers into its editorial workflow. In Locke's assessment, the eventual successful integration of computer technology into the manual world of the newsroom is attributed to the *Times* staff's extensive involvement, cooperation across departments, simultaneous development of the appropriate technology, and management's commitment of time and resources. In particular, the computerization of the newspaper was driven by the editorial department itself, not the technical team of the data processing staff, because the editorial staff better understood the needs of the newspaper and its mission. In other words, the conscious human efforts and choices relating to the newspaper's operations and vision, as well as the materiality of technology, drove effective computerization at the *Los Angeles Times*.[41]

Second, as shown in Mari's history of computerization, there was a nuanced engagement and appropriation of technology by news workers. For example, reporters were initially intimidated when VDTs were first introduced, but the news workers and management properly trained themselves for the new technology and used it to enhance their journalistic purpose. That is, although the technology was disruptive, it did not fundamentally challenge the existing journalistic norms of news workers. On the contrary, VDTs were helpful for efficient processing and journalistic autonomy, which helped them conduct more high-quality, original work (fig. 5). According to Mari, "this theme of the need to retain control, or domesticate technology

Figure 5 DEC VT-100, a popular video display terminal used in newsrooms, circa 1978. Photo: Flickr / Jason Scott (CC-BY-SA 2.0).

and tame it to use in newsrooms, reflects the pragmatic attitude many news workers felt about the introduction of new tools. Since they did not directly threaten their work patterns, only disrupted them (unlike mechanical workers, who felt more immediately in danger), reporters and editors tended to reskill on new devices in ways that empowered their sense of control over occupational boundaries."[42]

Overall, the adoption of computers in newsrooms followed several stages suggested by Amara's Law as well as other newsroom observers. News workers initially anticipate, fear, and disbelieve new tools. They then proceed to excitement for the new technology, only to be met with disillusionment and partial rejection. But with the realization of the technology's efficacy, which can help enhance journalistic norms, they rebound to enthusiasm for an innovative approach.[43]

This view of newsroom computerization from the perspective of news workers sketched here is important. Computerization has been studied by many journalism scholars, but the bulk of studies to date have focused on the effects of computerization on editorial processes and products—namely, how the reporters' information search and retrieval pattern has changed, how news content and format have been altered, and so on.[44] What is implied in such studies is the view that technology drives social change. As Pablo Boczkowski argues, "explicitly or by omission, this focus on technology's effects has espoused the notion that technological developments generate editorial effects."[45] But editorial effects are also the product of local newsroom dynamics, people, culture, and institutions, as the adaptive structuration theory suggests. As such, studying how news workers considered technology and how they voiced their hopes and frustrations—their agency—is meaningful.

The Internet, the Death of Newspapers, and New Journalistic Norms

The internet is often regarded as the printing press of the twentieth century. Those who have been living through the late twentieth and the early twenty-first centuries indeed are observing the power of the internet in every aspect of human affairs. Early scholarship about the internet's societal impact provided a rather utopian vision, where the previous power relationship is reversed and new forms of politics are experimented with, although some claimed that the internet was a medium controlled by the powerful and resourceful, where politics would operate as usual.[46] Similar arguments were produced in the domain of journalism scholarship: the internet's impact on news organizations was so massive that many news businesses that failed to adapt to the new media environment went bankrupt; furthermore, the internet gave birth to bloggers and citizen journalists who challenge the authority of professional journalism.

It is certainly true that many news organizations lost their advertising revenues to sites like Craigslist and went out of business. It is also true that we see instances in which powerful bloggers and citizen journalists changed the norms of professional journalism. However, understanding the extent to which these dynamics played out, as well as their underlying causes, requires a more thorough investigation. A close examination reveals that substantial changes in contemporary journalism have taken place, but the internet is not necessarily the deciding factor that has brought them about.

First, the common claim that the internet and the new media environment made the traditional news business, especially newspapers, not profitable anymore, and caused its collective demise, warrants a second look. It is indeed true that many newspapers have gone bankrupt since the late 1990s, exactly the time when the internet was starting to command a stronger presence in journalism. With the exceptions of giants such as the *New York Times* and the *Wall Street Journal*, most traditional medium- to small-scale local newspapers are either gone now or barely surviving. The estimated US daily newspaper circulation, print and digital combined, in 2018 was 28.6 million for weekday, a precipitous drop from 1990, when the pre-web-era circulation was more than 62 million.[47] The newspaper workforce declined from 458,000 people in 1990 to 183,000 people in 2016, almost a 60 percent drop, according to the US Bureau of Labor Statistics.[48] Such a decline in the newspaper business, the argument goes, resulted from the internet, which took away both advertising money as well as readers, who could find the content they wanted faster, easier, and more cheaply through the new medium.

But data suggest that the decline in the newspaper business in the United States began much earlier than the internet boom. Weekday newspaper circulation in the country peaked in 1984 at 63.3 million, and, since then, it has seen a downward spiral (see chart 1).[49] Considering the internet boom began in the late 1990s, it is difficult to say that it caused this steep decline in newspaper circulation. It is also informative to know that in a similar time frame, newspaper readership in Western Europe and Japan did not decline as sharply as in the United States.[50] Therefore, one can argue that it was more of a specific context of the United States that caused the fall, although the internet certainly fueled the trend.

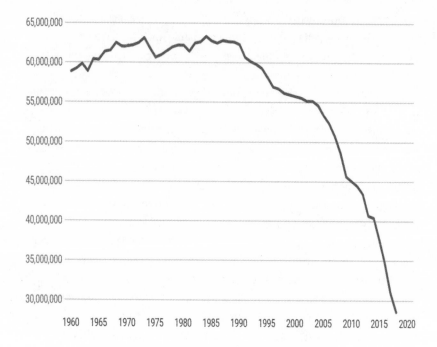

65,000,000

60,000,000

55,000,000

50,000,000

45,000,000

40,000,000

35,000,000

30,000,000

1960 1965 1970 1975 1980 1985 1990 1995 2000 2005 2010 2015 2020

Chart 1 Newspaper readership since 1960

So, what caused the decline of American newspapers? Some scholars argue that the problem with the American newspaper business was self-inflicted. According to Robert McChesney, one of the sharpest critics of the US media, unfettered American capitalism and corporate greed are the main culprits.[51] McChesney argues that large corporate chains since the 1980s gobbled up family-owned daily newspapers to generate higher profits. This was the time when the newspaper business was still profitable. Corporate chains bought the small newspapers, and, to generate even higher profits and satisfy investors, started producing low-quality, entertainment-oriented news, fired qualified journalists, and closed news bureaus. Indeed, by the end of the 1990s, the number of investigative reporters and foreign correspondents was slashed, and TV news programs were churning out dramatized stories based on police crime reports.[52] Diverse perspectives and quality stories were gone, and news became a form of cheap entertainment. This resulted in the public's disenchantment with journalism and general distrust of the news media. And that was the downfall of American journalism. It is worth listening to the testimony of David Simon, former *Baltimore Sun* reporter and creator of the famed HBO series *The Wire*, before the US Senate Subcommittee on Communications, Technology, and the Internet:

> When you hear a newspaper executive claiming that his industry is an essential bulwark of society and that it stands threatened by a new technology that is, as of yet, unready to shoulder the same responsibility, you may be inclined to empathize. And indeed, that much is true enough as it goes. But when that same newspaper executive then goes on to claim that this predicament has occurred through no fault on the industry's part, that they have merely been undone by new technologies, feel free to kick out his teeth. At that point, he's as fraudulent as the most self-aggrandized blogger.
>
> In fact, when newspaper chains began cutting personnel and content, their industry was one of the most profitable yet discovered by Wall Street money. We know now—because bankruptcy has opened the books—that *The Baltimore Sun* was eliminating its afternoon edition and trimming nearly 100 editors and reporters in an era when the paper was achieving 37 percent profits. In the years before the Internet deluge, the men and women who might have made *The Sun* a more essential vehicle for news and commentary—something so strong that it might have charged for its product online—they were being ushered out the door so that Wall Street could command short-term profits in the extreme. . . .
>
> In short, my industry butchered itself and we did so at the behest of Wall Street and the same unfettered, free-market logic that has proved so disastrous for so many American industries. And the original sin of American newspapering lies, indeed, in going to Wall Street in the first place.[53]

Another popular claim about the impact of the internet on journalism is that it significantly altered the industry's norms and practices: because the internet, characterized by openness and decentralization, allowed anyone to become a reporter, the gatekeeping and agenda-setting roles of professional journalism have been significantly undermined. Furthermore, bloggers and social media citizen activists have utilized interactive, transparent, and opinionated writing styles, which prompted changes in such traditional journalistic norms as objectivity, neutrality, and the separation of facts from opinions.

A wholesale argument that the internet completely changed the norms and practices of journalism may not be valid, but we do see significant changes here and there in the modern journalism universe. In terms of gatekeeping and agenda-setting, for example, the Black Lives Matter movement began on Twitter by citizen journalists and activists who filmed and distributed videos of police brutalities against unarmed Black civilians.[54] Similarly, the Occupy Wall Street protest was largely organized on social media and the internet. These movements seldom received mainstream media attention initially, but their concerted activism eventually caught the attention of the corporate media, suggesting a case of reverse agenda-setting from citizens to journalists.[55] In terms of journalistic norm changes, the freewheeling and opinionated style popular among bloggers and citizen journalists caught on in the mainstream media, and we now see the time-honored objectivity paradigm in journalism being dethroned as well.[56] Bloggers' writing often involves unhinged expressions of opinions, and it was important for them to be transparent by showing their sources through hyperlinks and disclosing biases (if any) publicly. This idea of transparency is now a principal norm of mainstream journalism adopted by the Society of Professional Journalists.[57]

These changes in journalistic norms and practices are by no means trivial. However, the degree to which they take place is perhaps not what the early internet enthusiasts had expected. The internet did not necessarily bring an overhaul in power relationships in the journalism world. Media giants in the pre-internet era such as the *New York Times*, CNN, the *Wall Street Journal*, and the *Washington Post* are still top sources of news today for most American news consumers. Despite the public's disenchantment with journalism, their news consumption is still dominated by mainstream media organizations that retain their role as "gatekeepers of what is credible and worthwhile rather than merely available."[58]

Furthermore, the adoption of new journalistic norms, such as transparency and interactivity, enabled by the new medium has been slow and sporadic. Whether it is a blog or Twitter, journalists generally normalized the new medium to fit their existing norms and practices. For example, in a study of journalist bloggers, Jane Singer found that journalists are still retaining their traditional gatekeeping role by incorporating little to no material from users, despite the inherently conversational and participatory nature of the blogging format.[59] Similarly, on microblogging platforms such as Twitter, where users are encouraged to express opinions and personal views in short bursts, it was found that journalists adapted Twitter's features to their existing norms. In particular, the journalists working for national newspapers and television news were less inclined than their counterparts working for less elite news outlets to relinquish their gatekeeping role in their tweets by sharing their stage with other news gatherers and commentators, or to provide accountability and transparency by providing information about their jobs, engaging in discussions with other tweeters, writing about their personal lives, or linking to external websites.[60]

More importantly, if there had been changes in journalistic norms and practices such that the press's gatekeeping role was undermined and the objectivity paradigm was broken, then the main force behind such changes were not necessarily the internet, although it certainly played a part. The underlying causes of the changes are more social and cultural. Modern journalism in America has long operated according to the old trustee model in which elitist reporters convey facts to the public. The reform of this model was long overdue. Ordinary citizens' disenchantment with and mistrust of the media, which they see as only catering to the elite and the powers that be, behind the facade of objectivity, already reached a peak in the late 1980s and early 1990s. Indeed, the media and the government have been the two entities that vie for the crown of the least trusted institution in the United States.[61] That's why reform movements in journalism, such as public journalism, began in the late 1980s and early 1990s, hoping to move journalism closer to the public it purports to serve. The rise of citizen journalism in the early 2000s was certainly propelled by the internet and social media, but what also lies behind it is citizens' desire to voice their own views, which are not covered by corporate media. It is a general trend of late modern democracy in which alienated citizens seek more participatory opportunities in society: from the Tea Party to the Occupy Wall Street movements, citizens who used to be alienated from politics under the elite-driven political and media system started forming their own coalitions and engaging in direct action.[62]

Another recent claim that faults the internet, and social media in particular, is the propagation of fake news and disinformation. Certainly, fake news flourishes on the internet because of the medium's open and decentralized nature. Anyone anywhere can easily manufacture fake news. But the root causes for the proliferation of fake news may lie elsewhere. Psychologically, people have a basic need to belong to a group. Some tend to share fake news despite knowing it is not true because, in doing so, they can affirm their identities and connect with others. They want to achieve a shared reality with other individuals and to gain acceptance in a social circle.[63] Not only that, but fake news also has cultural and historical context. In his compelling account, the novelist Kurt Andersen argues that the current explosion of fake news actually comes from the 1960s anti-science and anti-rationalism attitudes, along with America's fundamentalist religion, strong individualism, and the internet:

> America was created by true believers and passionate dreamers, and by hucksters and their suckers, which made America successful—but also by a people uniquely susceptible to fantasy, as epitomized by everything from Salem's hunting witches to Joseph Smith's creating Mormonism, from P. T. Barnum to speaking in tongues, from Hollywood to Scientology to conspiracy theories, from Walt Disney to Billy Graham to Ronald Reagan to Oprah Winfrey to Trump. In other words: mix epic individualism with extreme religion; mix show business with everything else; let all that ferment for a few centuries; then run it through the anything-goes '60s and the Internet age. The result is the America we inhabit today, with reality and fantasy weirdly and dangerously blurred and commingled.[64]

The internet, by all means, is a revolutionary technology. But it cannot be solely responsible for the demise of newspapers, shattered traditional journalistic norms and practices, and the proliferation of fake news. Its true impact on journalism and mass communication would require a more thorough examination of the technology's surrounding contexts and its interaction with them.

Virtual and Augmented Realities: The Empathy Machine?

In 2019, celebrating the fiftieth anniversary of the Apollo 11 moon landing, the *New York Times* did an interactive story in which readers could experience the event themselves. The creators pieced together the astronauts' original photos and transcripts into a condensed story. The sequence of the stacked photos and words gave viewers a sense of being there—the photos were projected into space and aligned with three-dimensional models of the moon terrain, giving a feel of the lunar environment. Viewers of the story could even walk in the astronauts' footsteps and manipulate a virtual camera to capture many of the iconic moonwalk images.[65] This was a prime example of how virtual reality (VR) and augmented reality (AR) technologies are applied to journalism to help readers better understand an event. Also, consider the 2017 PBS *Frontline* piece "After Solitary," in which viewers can walk around a tiny jail cell, experiencing what it is like to be solitarily confined.[66]

Solitary confinement is said to cause a slew of mental and behavioral problems for inmates, and for PBS viewers who have probably never been near jails, it was a great opportunity to vicariously taste a unique human experience, which may increase their empathy toward the inmates.

VR is a simulated experience of the real world in which individuals can interact within an artificial three-dimensional environment using electronic devices. Its close cousin, AR, refers to the enhancement of the real world using computer-generated perceptual information, such as overlaying digital imagery onto the real world. Taken together, they are known as "immersive technologies" that may completely change how we experience journalism. Their power lies in their transformative storytelling capabilities. They help provide viewers with a more accurate physical representation of space, spatial relationships, sense of spatial presence, and experienced immersion. The well-known VR film producer Chris Milk, who created a film that puts viewers inside a Syrian refugee camp, said the technology is an "ultimate empathy machine" that "connects humans to other humans in a profound way I've never before seen in any other form of media, and it can change people's perception of each other."[67] This statement is backed by some empirical research that suggests that VR can increase the empathy of viewers and their perception of the credibility of news.[68] That's why these technologies have been heralded as the new frontier of journalism. In fact, Goldman Sachs estimates that they will grow into a minimum $90 billion industry by 2025.[69]

These immersive technologies are indeed innovative. They change how we view the world and enhance our real-world experiences. They are now used to help surgeons practice delicate surgeries, customers envision home remodeling plans, and the military try out combat plans, to name a few. But beyond compelling applications in video gaming and marketing, it is difficult to say, at least for now, that VR and AR are successfully utilized in journalism. The *New York Times*, which heavily invested in VR and even handed out free VR headsets to subscribers, seems to be pulling away from it. Their once-famous VR mobile app is now gone, and their Daily 360 VR stories are only sporadically updated. *USA Today* and the *Guardian* once led the way in VR by establishing a dedicated VR production unit. But their initiative has stalled, too. *USA Today*'s ambitious "VRtually There" stories ceased to appear after 2018. In terms of AR, the prospects appear to be somewhat better because production using AR can be slightly easier and the experience is more user-friendly than VR. The *New York Times* produced some compelling AR stories, such as how an emergency crew rescued a boys' soccer team trapped in a cave in Thailand, which helped viewers experience how dangerous the rescue mission was. Industry-wide, however, good AR stories are still scant.

What's happening to the touted next frontier of journalism? The immersive technologies do not seem to be taking off, and they may never fulfill the rosy promises journalism technologists made years ago. There are several reasons for this. First, it should be noted that these technologies have a long history and went through cycles of hype and disillusionment, as did most other technologies. And they are still going through these cycles, suggesting that it will still be some time before they find meaningful traction in journalistic applications.

In terms of general VR history, the filmmaker Morton Heilig in 1962 created the Sensorama, dubbed as the "cinema of the future" (fig. 6). It was probably the first true VR system and consisted of a big box with a 3D display, vibrating seat, and scent producer. A couple of years later, the computer scientist Ivan Sutherland created the first head-mounted VR system that rendered images for the viewer's changing pose. Expensive and heavy like industrial machines, these technologies failed to take off. In the 1970s and '80s, the commercial application of VR was rare, but research was active in universities and institutes. In the late '80s, the computer scientist and philosopher Jaron Lanier coined the term "virtual reality," and his lab developed a range of VR gear and the first commercial VR goggles; around the same time, NASA started using VR to train astronauts. Still, the VR goggles and gloves at the time cost at least $10,000 apiece and mass adoption was inconceivable. In the 1990s, VR and AR development and adoption took a new turn with their applications in gaming. Although very crude by today's standards, they excited many gamers and popularized the technologies to an extent. As we enter the twenty-first century, the development and adoption of the technology is still slow, but the hype is real. Google started selling the much-touted AR device Google Glass in 2013 at the more manageable price of $1,500, but it failed to reach wide adoption and was discontinued shortly after the launch (fig. 7). In 2014, Facebook bought the Oculus VR platform for $2 billion, an obvious sign that the social network giant saw a future in VR. In 2016, the gimmicky AR game *Pokémon Go* excited many people worldwide, but it fizzled as quickly as it emerged. The continued success of VR/AR still seems difficult to achieve.

The history of immersive technology's use in journalism is much shorter and filled with more failures than successes. Probably the first case of VR journalism appeared in 2010, when a team of journalists created an animation that gave users the experience of being in an interrogation room in an

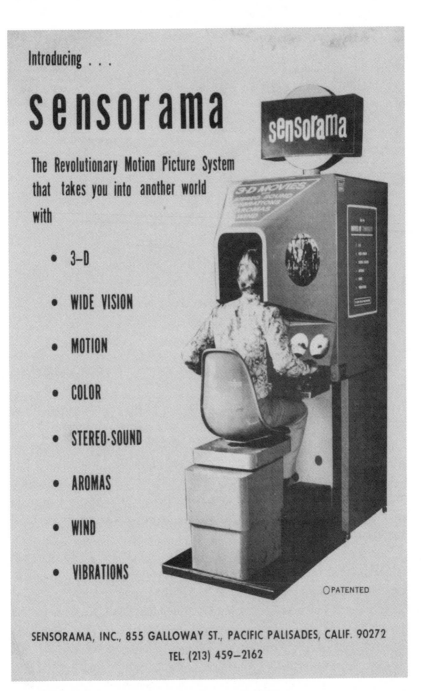

Figure 6 Sensorama advertisement, circa 1962. Photo © Morton Heilig, courtesy of USC School of Cinematic Arts, Hugh M. Hefner Moving Image Archive.

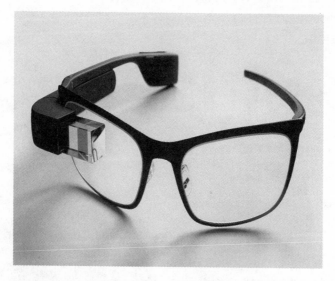

Figure 7 Google Glass, first edition, 2013. Photo: Wikimedia Commons / Mike Panhu (CC-BY-SA 3.0).

offshore prison.[70] This was followed by serious attempts from mainstream news organizations such as the *New York Times*, CNN, the *Guardian*, and *USA Today*. But as mentioned above, their immersive stories are today hard to come by. And the few available immersive stories are mostly limited to such subjects as travel, nature, and sports. For example, a glimpse at current VR stories at *USA Today* and the *Guardian* revealed the following titles: "Indy Car Racing," "Wilderness," "The Joy of Frogs," and "Soar in Hot Air Balloon over New Mexico." It may need some time before these technologies are effectively used for breaking news events. It would also require careful long-term research on user reception.

Even with careful long-term research, how much the technologies can be useful in journalism is still unclear. Skeptics argue that humans are analog beings and a VR camera cannot bridge the gap between near and far because the analog measure between near and far is always too far for the human scale and cognitive faculties to fully connect with through mediation.[71] No matter how good the technologies become, VR news will always be a substitute for actually being in the presence of the actual events. This is less of an issue in video gaming because gamers will understand that the sophisticated virtual world is just that, a virtual world for gaming. But in news that is supposed to depict reality, this inherent paradox of VR looms larger. As Robert Hassan argues, "The VR commodity spectacle is fundamentally just that: a sophisticated camera apparatus that produces an integrated spectacle; a capacity to stupefy through an immersive representation that is technological prior to being virtual—and where reality does not and cannot play its part, except as a representation of a distant spatial and temporal event."[72]

What makes VR/AR even more difficult in journalistic applications is the fact that there are few to no accepted standards or norms for their use in news reporting. These technologies have great potential for manipulation.[73] In VR/AR, fake news may become more real, and with their supposedly increased credibility and empathy dimensions, viewers may be more easily manipulated. In a way, the current VR journalists are akin to the first generation of photojournalists in the nineteenth century. The early photojournalists, hauling around heavy, cumbersome, and expensive equipment, had to set the scene or even stage the scenes to compose compelling photos. In a famous incident, for instance, the French photographer Ernest Eugène Appert in 1871 faked a massacre scene to brutally portray a certain political group. His photographs were carefully curated and emotionally laden for propaganda purposes.[74] Likewise, using heavy, expensive production equipment and faced with numerous opportunities to get involved in constructing the scenes, today's VR/AR journalists face many ethical dilemmas.[75]

VR/AR production gears will eventually become cheaper and more manageable in the near future. But it took decades of debates to establish what we today call acceptable ethics and practices of photojournalism. It is also likely that we will need a significant amount of time and laborious effort to establish a social compact regarding the ethical use of immersive technologies. A case in point here is the South Korean documentary *Meeting You*, in which producers reunited a grieving mother with her dead daughter through VR.[76] It was a spectacle. Millions of viewers were engrossed and became highly emotional at the scene in which the mother touches her daughter, who comes alive through VR. However, it caused a heated controversy: Is it ethically acceptable to force-generate feelings through VR, for both the mother and the viewers? Will there be any long-term psychological effects on the part of the mother when she returns to the real world? Was there an increase in empathy on the part of the viewers, and if so, was it genuine? Overall, what is the acceptable use of the VR technology in storytelling? These are the questions that need to be discussed and answered through a societal discourse. Social norms and ethics matter for the meaningful adoption and use of technologies.

Last but not least, a viable business model is a must for the immersive technologies to take off in journalistic applications. VR/AR applications have been successful in the gaming industry because gamers were willing to pay a premium for more lifelike simulations. But the journalism industry is still trying to figure out how to monetize VR/AR, and the answer to that is not easy to come by. Would readers pay more for more lifelike news content that would bring them closer to the action? Given the current state of journalism, in which news organizations have trouble finding customers willing to pay even a small amount of money for good reporting, VR/AR content that will typically require much higher costs and resources in production will not likely pay off. According to some journalists, one way to deal with this issue of commercial reality is to produce "branded content" or advertiser-sponsored news.[77] But would viewers want native advertisements following themselves in the virtual world whenever they tilt their heads and change directions? How would that affect the news pieces' credibility and viewers' empathy that VR is supposed to produce? Currently, no good revenue model exists for the immersive technologies' use in journalism. Innovative technology alone cannot generate needed changes or improvements in journalism. As shown in the case of the printing press, where modern capitalism and literacy were preconditions for its development and adoption, viable commercial structures and business models are needed for immersive technologies to take off in journalism.

Will Artificial Intelligence Save or Destroy Journalism?

If I can provide a crude and blunt answer to the question posed in the subheading above, the answer would be "neither." Artificial intelligence (AI) is not going to save journalism, nor will it destroy it. This does not mean that AI's impact on journalism is minimal. On the contrary, AI's effects are being felt very strongly. Its power and reach over journalism are probably more extensive than any other contemporary technology. Like all other domains of society affected by the increasingly ubiquitous presence of AI, journalism is being transformed by this powerful technology. But the discourse surrounding the industry tends to be simplistic and binary: AI will displace human reporters; AI will emancipate reporters from chores of newsroom labor and elevate them to do more value-added work; AI and sophisticated algorithms will trap readers in the filter bubble or echo chamber of like-minded people and opinions. These positions are seldom supported by empirical reality. They arise from either panic or hyperbole about technology. They tend to disregard the nuanced and detailed interactions occurring between technology and people that may produce complex results.

Although artificial intelligence is one of the top social concerns today, its origin goes back to the 1950s. And its not-so-short history suggests that rosy promises and fearful concerns have dominated the narrative surrounding the technology, overshadowing its actual capabilities.[78] The event that founded AI as a formal field of research was the Dartmouth Summer Research Project on Artificial Intelligence in 1956, where leading mathematicians and cognitive scientists of the time gathered for a summer. When the academic idea was introduced to the public shortly thereafter, there was much hype. The media and general public imagined that the scientists were creating an awesome thinking machine that was "smarter than people, unlimited, fast, mysterious, and frightening."[79] Popular science magazines during this early development of AI helped construct a powerful cultural myth such that the thinking machine would be able to perfectly simulate the cognitive faculties of the human mind and that the present shortcomings would shortly be overcome.[80] A sentient AI was deemed imminent. But advances were slow and the field soon entered the "AI winter," a long period of reduced interest and funding in the subject. The AI winter was also a result of overinflated promises and high expectations.[81] In the second decade of the twenty-first century, however, it really looks like AI is coming to fruition to some extent because of the availability of big data and super-fast processing units. AI has now conquered the game of Go, which was considered impossible for a long time, and is increasingly doing things that had been imagined only in science fiction. Our modern social fabric is being constructed more and more in a vast data universe where AI does the groundwork. But more ubiquitous and generalized use of AI will take much longer. The Dartmouth Workshop of 1956 produced most of the AI concepts we talk about today. The scientists had thought they would produce significant advances in one summer, but their prediction was completely off. As one data scientist observed, "We thought it would be one grad student over one summer, and it turns out to be dozens of research labs over sixty years."[82] And after such a long time, the most dominant forms of AI employed today are machine learning, natural language generation, pattern recognition, and computer vision. These are not really part of "artificial general intelligence," or a machine that can think for itself and engage in abstract reasoning (i.e., a thinking machine). Bluntly speaking, the current AI forms are just more advanced and sophisticated statistical techniques based on big data. It is statistics and data processing on steroids.

Still, AI's impact on society and journalism is immense. It is true that there is still a high degree of hype about AI today, but its effects are real. AI is influencing all the important dimensions of journalism: newsgathering, production, and distribution. For example, machine learning helps reporters mine datasets for insights; natural language generation is used in news production to turn data into text; in news distribution, AI is used in such tasks as news personalization and comment moderation. In short, AI is already widely used in news organizations, big or small. But is it driving human reporters to extinction? Is it liberating journalists? Is it trapping the readers in the cocoon of like-minded people? Barely. First, growing evidence suggests that AI is likely to augment journalists rather than replace them. While AI is replacing the routinized work of reporting stock prices and sports scores, it is also creating new work—it requires plenty of people in journalism who can develop, adjust, validate, supervise, and monitor the AI systems.[83] If journalists are freed from tedious stock price reporting work, then it can be argued that they may channel their newfound time and energy to a higher order of journalistic work, such as investigative reporting. But does that mean reporters are being liberated? On the contrary, the new work routines created by AI and the skills to be developed to utilize the technology mean more occupational pressure and labor. It has been shown that conducting high-impact investigative journalism using AI or computational techniques is a very time- and resource-consuming endeavor, often costing a large amount of money and several months.[84] Even developing a relatively simple automated photo tagging system is not an easy task. AP journalists reported that their photo tagging system required a lot of personnel—both technical and journalistic—and a couple of years, and they still had to supervise the system, manually approving the suggested tags for each image.[85] So, rather than destroying or saving journalism, AI is most likely changing how things are organized and conducted to varying degrees.

Lastly, the argument that readers are trapped in the filter bubble generated by AI algorithms has been disputed in many academic studies.[86] What the recent research suggests is that the savvy digital public today, with their multiple and overlapping identities and diverse networks, are keenly aware of different viewpoints surrounding them, and their media diets tend to include at least some disagreements and challenging perspectives. And even if the filter bubble / echo chamber does occur and threatens the healthy functioning of democracy, its root causes are not so much algorithms as social and political contexts. It is more human choice and desire that create the filter bubble, although filtering algorithms exacerbate it.[87]

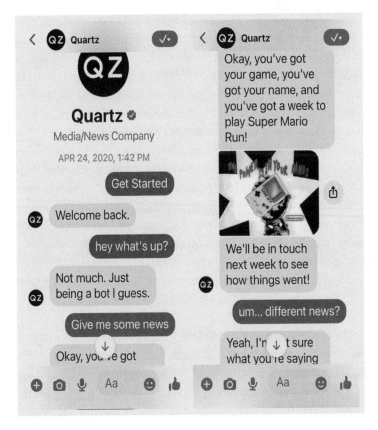

Figure 8 Chatbot from *Quartz*. Photo: author.

The adoption of AI is also moderated, or facilitated, by the larger dynamics of news institutions. One recent example illustrates how AI adoption is processed through journalistic organizational forces: the so-called chatbots, or conversational news agents powered by natural language processing of AI, which were all the rage among news organizations between 2015 and 2018 (see fig. 8 for an example of a chatbot). Top news organizations such as CNN, *Quartz*, and Condé Nast developed chat systems, especially aimed at young users, whom they believe to be the future of news consumption. As of 2021, however, it seems that most news organizations have abandoned chatbots. What happened to this once-popular technology? There are several reasons why this technology failed to be widely adopted, including a lack of functionality and the young audience's quickly fading interest. But another important reason from the side of news organizations is that the innovation has been stymied because of conflicting institutional logics within the newsroom.

According to Valerie Belair-Gagnon and colleagues, chatbots were developed and operated by newsroom "intrapreneurs," or entrepreneurs developed within existing organizations, with the corporate logic of experimentation, audience orientation, and efficiency-seeking, but such an approach clashed with a journalistic logic prioritizing news workflows, formats, and autonomy for news workers. That is, too often chatbots were not in sync with traditional news formats, which made it difficult for reporters to follow up on stories and develop sustained conversations using chatbots, or with news delivery, which relegated chatbots to the status of "add-ons" rather than vital tools. Hence, these clashing logics limited the chatbots' adoption and influence.[88] This finding is in line with what the adaptive structuration theory predicted: that structures in technology and structures in institutions and human actions are continually intertwined, shaping each other.[89] In the case of chatbots, "this tension revealed how the corporate logics of newsbots enjoyed management support as desirable in their own right, but the professional features of newsbots created constraints that were too hard to overcome when attempted in regular news production."[90]

At the end of the day, AI will not likely change the fundamentals of journalism. The current application of AI in journalism usually involves story generation, which is just a use of different narrative styles based on templates, and some sort of machine learning to find patterns from big data. It cannot interpret facts from different angles, negotiate with sources, formulate informed opinions, or apply insights to other contexts—the essence of good journalism. The current AI systems work best with neatly organized and highly structured datasets. But human experiences are heavily individualized webs of subtle causes and effects, sometimes unpredictable and erratic, and are not easily reduced to structured data. Understanding them requires human journalists' judgment, interpretation, creativity, and empathy. It is not likely that AI will ever possess such capabilities.

Is Blockchain a New Savior of Journalism?

Blockchain is riding high as the latest iteration of technological hype. Despite the technology's complex and ambiguous nature, it has entered lay vocabulary due to the popularity of such applications as Bitcoin. Blockchain is an amalgam of many things and is not easily defined; for most people, exactly how it operates is even more difficult to comprehend. At a minimum, blockchain is a record-keeping database where data are saved in a "chain of blocks" on a network of computers spread across the world. The stored data are immutable and secure. Bernat Ivancsics at the Tow Center for Digital Journalism labels it a special kind of Wikipedia: many people can edit a single database, and all edits are tracked. But unlike Wikipedia, once a new chunk of data (or block) is added to the database, it cannot be edited, and everyone in the network keeps a copy of the entire blockchain for themselves; there is no centralized, shared database, and edits can't be tracked by clicking on an "Edit History" button. Instead of rewriting the same page or database, blockchain is cumulative—or in other words, append-only.[91]

The most well-known application of blockchain to date is cryptocurrency, especially Bitcoin. Whenever a Bitcoin transaction takes place, an army of computers on the Bitcoin blockchain network verifies the transaction to make sure it is legitimate, and then the transaction is recorded in the immutable and distributed ledger. Exactly how it does that is a complex mathematical operation known as "hashing." Those who engage in the verification and auditing work using their computers are also known as "miners," because, in doing so, they can get rewarded with (or mine) Bitcoins (see fig. 9). Blockchain is a disruptive and innovative technology because it

Figure 9 Cryptocurrency mining farm equipped with high-powered computers. Photo: Flickr / Marko Ahtisaari (CC-BY-SA 2.0).

From the Printing Press to Blockchain

makes it possible to perform transactions without involving a central authority—in the case of Bitcoin, the authority would be a bank. The *Economist* thus called the technology a "trust machine," which lets individuals who have no particular confidence in each other collaborate.[92] And this feature has the potential to transform the economy in important ways.

The application of blockchain in journalism comes in many ways. One of the more popular and intuitive uses for news organizations is to store articles and their metadata within a secure blockchain ledger, rather than storing them on their content management system or other third-party servers. The usual information that will be stored on a blockchain includes articles' timestamps, copyright, and authorship, which will help reporters' and freelancers' claims about their intellectual property and potentially prevent plagiarism. Second, blockchain and its cryptocurrency system may help improve the news business model. Readers can utilize cryptocurrency to pay for a subscription or tip a reporter. They can also earn cryptocurrency by interacting with news content like commenting on and fact-checking stories. Even reporters' salaries can be paid by cryptocurrency, thereby making the reporters shareholders of the system. Low transaction costs associated with cryptocurrency make this economic model viable. Third, blockchain and its application, known as "smart contracts," can be used for newsroom governance and other journalistic purposes. A smart contract is a legal agreement codified into computer code that automatically triggers when particular conditions are met and that cannot be tempered once implemented. A smart contract can be a financial arrangement, a lease, or, in the case of decentralized newsrooms on a blockchain network, a voting system that governs the process of newsroom operations.

The highest-profile example to date is Civil, the journalism blockchain platform that operated based on its own cryptocurrency, and also on the smart contract-based Constitution, a governance system that allowed members to vote on the ethical and journalistic standards of newsrooms. Civil began with much fanfare and hype in 2016, going public with an ICO (initial coin offering) in 2018. But it struggled for much of its existence and folded operations in June 2020. A closer look at what happened to Civil reveals the promise and peril of technology in journalism.

Upon its launch, Civil developers and supporters argued that their system could increase reader trust through transparency of authorship and accreditation as well as through the Constitution, which guaranteed ethical journalistic standards. It could also generate new streams of revenue for newsrooms based on cryptocurrency, according to Civil leaders.[93] In other words, Civil blockchain claimed it could handle the issues of trust and finance, the two fundamental problems of contemporary journalism.

Civil and other emerging blockchain journalism initiatives may really help solve journalism's chronic problems. We should try whatever we can to regain the public's trust in journalism and develop a more sustainable news business model. But much like AI, the narrative surrounding blockchain in journalism is that of a technological silver bullet, where the technology is considered to be the ultimate solution to the industry's ills. Can the blockchain technology become the savior of journalism when most of journalism's problems are nontechnological? As noted above, many of American journalism's problems come from the industry itself. The public's trust of media collapsed due to their profit-driven reporting, miscalled election results, and sensational fearmongering. Can blockchain really solve those problems? Probably not. These ills are internal and tied to the issues of unfettered late modern capitalism. Blockchain may help, but it does not get at the heart of the problems. Some of the newsrooms that flourished on the Civil blockchain network, such as the *Colorado Sun* and *Sludge*, have been successful primarily due to their independent, in-depth, on-the-ground reporting, not due to the technology per se. Readers of such news would pay for and invest in good content, regardless of whether blockchain was involved. Let's take a close look at the *Colorado Sun*. After multiple layoffs, former employees of the legacy daily *Denver Post* founded the *Colorado Sun* with the help of a Civil grant in 2018.[94] In its less than two years on the Civil platform, the paper received multiple awards for its in-depth coverage of vital issues in Colorado.[95] But the funding from Civil dried up and the paper appeared to be in a financial crisis. Then the paper converted to a membership model and readers stepped forward in a big way.[96] How did this small newspaper successfully convert to a membership model? Because its journalism was good. What was Civil's role there? What Civil mainly did was to provide necessary start-up grants to the *Colorado Sun*. Civil's blockchain technology was barely a factor in the newspaper's success.

Many of blockchain's promises—such as increased transparency through an open and immutable database, rewarding active members of the community, and maintaining ethical journalistic standards—can be achieved without the technology or cryptocurrency itself. Some may even be better handled without the complex technological system. Take the case of the smart contract–enabled voting, for example. Civil argued that its token (cryptocurrency)–holding members can challenge a newsroom or stories that violate their ethical standards by staking a token deposit. The community will then vote, using their token, to decide whether the newsroom in question violated the Civil Constitution. This convoluted mechanism attempts to impose hard rules on very subjective issues like ethics, which are open to interpretation. Perhaps a better alternative to decide on the ethical standards of journalism would be for the members to just talk it out the old-fashioned way.

Smart contracts like the one Civil operated on are littered with problems. Blockchain researcher David Gerard points out that smart contracts are based on a severely limited understanding of how contracts, the law, and social agreements work: smart contracts concentrate on a technical form that can be put into computer code and do not address the social meaning of what a contract is, the changeable contexts real-world contracts operate in, and how they are fulfilled in practice.[97] In the real world, human behavior is not easily codified in digital contracts. Such was the case with TruStory, another blockchain-based media company. On the now-defunct platform, users could stake tokens to write an argument, which then would get voted on by other users. If the argument attracted positive "upvotes," the original staker would win a bonus.[98] This type of system incentivizes users to behave tactically and collusively, encouraging them to write only arguments with which other users would agree. Now compare TruStory to Reddit, a similar, and much more successful, discussion platform. Reddit does not use any monetary reward system like cryptocurrency or any other advanced technologies. The reason it is successful is mainly because of its simplicity, user-friendliness, and the enthusiasm of its members.[99]

Perhaps blockchain is more useful as an idea than as a technology. According to critically informed researchers of the technology, blockchain is a powerful cultural and political product that has emerged from the crisis of the neoliberal economy: it derives its legitimacy and authority from the promises of radical transparency and decentralization in a world where global financial concentration produces severe inequalities.[100] That is, the problems of modern society gave power to blockchain, not the other way around. The same goes for journalism. The inherent problems of modern journalism and its deep desire to reinvent itself gave validity to the idea of blockchain. But lots of people in the journalism industry today don't know what to do with the blockchain technology, because they don't have clear aims or vision. Without proper understanding, research, and plans, they just feel the imperative to go along with the latest technology. As such, blockchain in journalism as it currently stands is used more as a marketing tool. As blockchain researcher Lana Swartz said, "the blockchain is more useful as a rhetorical strategy than technological strategy."[101]

Looking at the long history as well as currently developing cases of technology's relationship to journalism, it becomes clear that technology is "only one element in a dialectical process" that includes such other factors as economics, cultural values, and political movements.[102] It should also be noted that these technologies were not invented specifically for journalistic purposes: Gutenberg and Samuel Morse did not create their inventions thinking about newspapers; the internet began as a military-scientific network; the origins of VR are related to entertainment and cinema; AI was a scientific computing project; blockchain began as a ledger for secure financial transactions online. It was human agency that gave them purpose and meaning for journalism.

There will be more interesting and disruptive technologies to come. Some may fail and some may succeed. But if media history is any guide to understanding future disruptions, it shows that "tech tools rarely lead directly to a clear, dark dystopia or an obvious, euphoric utopia. Reflecting the rest of reality, it is a bit of both."[103] The history also teaches us that those processes will be piecemeal, full of dashed hopes and slow development, conditioned by social forces.

Understanding the complex historical relationship between journalism and technology informs journalism insiders as well as the broader public about what the future holds for society. Journalism has always been connected to democracy and public life.[104] Healthy democracy requires well-functioning journalism. How technological innovations affect (or do not affect) journalism, and what kind of journalism we will have as a result, is an important matter for a sustainable democratic society. As Patricia Dooley observes, "Journalists and technologies do not exist in a vacuum, and being well informed about journalism's historical relationship to technology puts us in a better position to be fully engaged in the construction of a better future."[105]

The Journalistic Field and the Narrative of Techno-Journalism

> Give me a laboratory and I will raise a world.
>
> —Bruno Latour

"If you are a journalism educator or media professional, I have news for you: We work in tech," a journalism professor declared.[1] This claim is not an exaggeration. It is difficult to deny the importance of technology in today's journalism. After all, many newsrooms have disappeared, failing to adapt to the new digital media landscape, while some tech-savvy news organizations have made strides. Contemporary newsroom management constantly seeks shiny new innovations that may boost their sagging profits, while reporters are asked to be equipped with sophisticated technological skills and regularly attend technology workshops.

Even powerful legacy newsrooms, such as the *New York Times*, have struggled to remain relevant in this techno-journalism world. The newspaper's leaked *Innovation* report in 2014 showed how desperate it was to catch up with the latest technological innovations.[2] In that internal report, the venerable newspaper lamented its digital shortcomings against what it called "competitors," such as *BuzzFeed*, *Business Insider*, and the *Huffington Post*, and argued for constant innovation. The tone of the report was that of anxiety—a fear that it might lag behind in the fast-evolving digital world. Such angst is also confirmed by Nikki Usher, who did an ethnographic study of the *Times* newsroom. Her work shows that *Times* journalists worried about becoming irrelevant if they could not keep the web up to date, fearing they might not be a comprehensive and all-inclusive source of information.[3]

This chapter takes a close look at reporters' and news organizations' attitudes toward technologies in newswork and analyzes their discourse about technology in journalism. It tries to explain why and how a technology-driven narrative is dominant in journalism circles. Utilizing Pierre Bourdieu's field theory as a general theoretical framework, this chapter discusses how the professional journalistic field, which is rapidly losing its jurisdictional control, attempts to reassert its boundaries using technological means.

The Unstable Journalistic Field

What would be the best way to produce a good medical reporter? Would training an existing reporter with medical knowledge and sending her to work on a medical beat be enough? How about hiring an actual doctor and training her as a reporter? Which way is more effective, and how would the audience perceive their credibility as a reporter? How about science, economic, and legal reporters? Would news organizations prefer training reporters as experts in science, economics, and law to hiring actual scientists, economists, and lawyers and training them as reporters?

Decades ago, when journalists in the United States maintained a relatively authoritative position as producers of knowledge and information, the answers to the questions above were easy: reporters were groomed to become experts on their chosen beats, and they maintained a degree of autonomy from other professions. Currently, however, few people can say that with confidence. It is not uncommon today to observe scientists and doctors engaging in journalism, both within and outside news organizations. Competent citizens also engage in journalistic work on the subjects they are passionate about, challenging the authority of professional journalism. Various political regulations and economic pressures on journalism are growing as well. In other words, the journalistic field has a crisis in its jurisdictional control.

To better understand why the journalism industry pursues technological innovation relentlessly, journalism's relationship with other spheres of society, as well as its internal functioning, needs close examination. Here, the French sociologist Pierre Bourdieu's field theory comes in handy to analyze the complex dynamics of the journalistic field vis-à-vis others. Field theory has gained gradual yet strong acceptance among American scholars who study the sociology of news. Bourdieu himself applied his initial idea of the field to journalism, and American scholars such as Rodney Benson expanded its efficacy for the study of journalism.[4]

To briefly overview field theory, some major concepts need to be explicated: *field*, *doxa*, *habitus*, *capital*, and *autonomy*. A *field* is where competitions among social agents take place to preserve or transform the occupational space. It may be defined as "a network or a configuration of objective relations between positions."[5] Politics is a field, and so is medicine, economics, and law. There are smaller or subfields, such as accounting, various musical genres, and academic disciplines. Journalism is a field as well with its own rules and norms. The rules and norms unique to a certain field are known as *doxa*, or, in Bourdieu's words, "a universe of tacit presuppositions that organize action within the field."[6] In the journalistic field, such norms as objectivity and rules about news judgment constitute its doxa. *Habitus* is what links the individual and the social, and it is Bourdieu's take on the foundational concept of sociology: agency versus structure. "To speak of habitus is to assert that the individual and even the personal, the subjective, is social, collective. Habitus is socialized subjectivity," Bourdieu declared.[7] The notion of habitus expresses the idea that individuals' predispositions, assumptions, judgments, and behaviors are the result of a long-term process of socialization.[8] *Capital* refers to various forms of resources available within a field. According to field theory, there are two main forms of capital: economic and cultural. Economic capital simply means money and assets, whereas cultural capital encompasses educational credentials, technical expertise, general knowledge, and artistic sensibilities. A field maintains its *autonomy* by accumulation and preservation of capital. For a field like journalism, cultural capital is particularly important, because it provides the respect and authority necessary to maintain the field's autonomy.

Field theory emphasizes interrelationship among actors. Within and across fields, relations of power fundamentally structure human actions. Actors within social fields accrue capital unique to their own fields and may exercise force on other actors. Individuals and groups are thus in a constant struggle to preserve, expand, or transform their fields. The same happens across fields, such that they pull and push against one another. In doing so, some social fields may overlap with or even blur into others.

The relational perspective present in field theory is important because it allows us to think of journalism as a dynamic process of professional practices. Traditionally, professions have been defined based on traits, such as credentials, expertise, ethics, and culture.[9] Journalism, too, has often been considered a trait-based profession, subscribing to the ideals of journalistic ethics and norms, and pronouncing specific claims to authority over a body of a social function.[10] But compared to such traditional professions as law and medicine, journalism does not have as strong or established traits. After all, you don't need a license to become a reporter. This is why some wonder whether journalism is a profession at all, or regard it as a quasi-profession, where its professional expertise is "parasitic" in the sense that journalists have expertise in another field.[11] But more recent sociological research suggests that a trait-based approach to the idea of a profession is limited and outdated because it does not account for how a profession develops and gains control over work-related tasks, and how it wards off intrusion from other social groups into its field.[12] Therefore, it is useful to move away from trait-based assessments of a profession to considerations of the social functions of a type of occupation. Under this "process" approach, whether or not journalism is a profession is of less importance. What's more important is what it does in society and how it plays its roles. As Nikki Usher argues, the dynamics of journalism may be better understood not as a profession but as a process of knowledge construction and as continuous creation and re-creation of practices and jurisdictional claims.[13] The same goes for Silvio Waisbord, who suggests journalism is not a profession but a social field complete with its own doxa and capital. Based on Bourdieu's field theory, Waisbord reimagines journalism as a social field always in flux, where the invisible relations of social, cultural, political, and economic forces are intertwined. He suggests that journalistic professionalism is defined not so much by traits and credentials as by a social and occupational jurisdiction where journalists strive to retain the autonomy to control their work according to internal rules and practices of news production and dissemination.[14]

Having sketched field theory, why journalism is so fixated on the idea of technological innovation can be explained by analyzing both the inside and the outside of the journalistic field. Internally, the journalistic field is faced with constant economic pressure to stay afloat and generate profits. The journalistic field is composed of economic capital, expressed through circulation, advertising revenues, and audience ratings, and cultural capital, expressed through in-depth reporting and intelligent commentaries. But the journalistic field's cultural capital, as Bourdieu suggests, is weaker than its own economic capital, as well as compared to the cultural capital of such other fields as art and literature. The modern journalistic field is characterized more by economic capital, and thus it is a very weak autonomous field that can hardly stand on its own.[15] This means that the field is highly susceptible to economic and other pressures. Of course, commercial motives have always dominated the journalistic field, especially in the United States, but their power is even further growing in these times of increased market competition. The balance between economic and cultural capital has become more tilted in favor of the former. This powerful economic logic inside the field compels increased innovation tied to profit generation. Indeed, many recent technologies appropriated in journalism are about monitoring audience behaviors and turning them into measurable assets, such as increased web traffic and audience engagement. New media platforms and associated journalistic practices are often developed by considering financial motives, trying to include new target audiences for advertisers.[16] Edson Tandoc's newsroom observation study tells a similar tale. Tandoc suggests that journalists adopt and use web analytics technologies to inform their strategies to increase traffic, and this is an important sign that journalists regard the audience as a form of capital. Faced with the reality of sagging profits for traditional journalism, journalists clearly perceive capital instability within the journalistic field. This instability has opened up the gates to the influence of the audience, conceived of by journalists as largely a form of economic capital that can be maximized to preserve fiscal stability in the journalistic field, according to Tandoc.[17] To sum it up, the relatively weak cultural capital in the journalistic field is being increasingly appropriated by its economic counterpart, which drives the discourse of technological innovation for economic survival and improvement. Following the internal economic imperative, journalists are asked to accumulate technological skills and expertise to allow the field to "increase its economic capital in the long run, with rising output, lower costs, and higher profits."[18]

Within the journalistic field, technological innovation and expertise are also sought after because of a desire to remain relevant and keep its autonomy. As argued above, journalism's status as a profession is not as established as others, and its mode of operation—building specialized knowledge based on others' expertise—is currently under threat. Therefore, the field has an urgent need to reclaim its authority over information and knowledge. Usher's recent study attests to this point.[19] In an ethnography of major US newsrooms, Usher studied the incorporation of "hacker journalists" into news organizations. Hacker journalists are those who possess computer coding capabilities. Usher's study suggests that hacker journalists are needed—welcomed, actually—in news organizations to create something new in order to help journalism change and meet the needs of the digital conditions it faces. To keep exerting its influence, the journalistic field requires new ways of thinking about and doing journalism, and hacker journalists help push the field forward. These hacker journalists, according to Usher, did not meet with strong resistance from the existing actors of the field; rather, they were subsumed into the overriding practices of the larger profession. Exactly how they were bought into the norms of journalism depends on their habitus—their origins, education, social and cultural backgrounds—such that the programmer-to-journalist socialization is different from that of the journalists who taught themselves programming. Overall, however, most of them got acquainted with and followed the doxa of the journalistic field. As Usher found out, even though some of the technologists did not necessarily identify themselves as "journalists," they understood the editorial workflow, demands, needs, and expectations of newsrooms and communicated according to journalistic norms. Eventually, they expanded the professional jurisdiction over work and knowledge for journalism, and, therefore, the hacker journalists' story as a subfield in journalism is "one of acceptance and welcome rather than threat and fear."[20] This welcoming trend of technologists in journalism is quite a turnaround compared to the traditional newsrooms of the recent past. Not too long ago, technologists—designers, coders, developers—were deemed inferior to reporters in terms of newsroom status. They were considered more like support staff who were not engaged in "real" journalistic work. Today, their status is quite high in newsrooms, as observed in their elevated pay and their increasingly strong command of expertise and control in content production.

That new technologists, such as hacker journalists, entered and operated in the journalistic field without strong resistance is in line with field theory's prediction that despite the inherent dynamism and conflict inside the field, most of the new entrants' activities will largely reproduce the structure of the field.[21] This is a consistent finding: a similar observation was made by Wilson Lowrey, who studied artists and designers in newsrooms. He found that although many "visual journalists" came from the art world with non-journalistic backgrounds, they tended to align with overarching journalistic norms.[22] This is because an entry into the journalistic field requires "acceptance of the basic rules of the game, which themselves are a powerful force of inertia."[23] These hacker journalists, visual journalists, and technologists understand the inner working of newsrooms and largely follow the norms and principles of the journalistic field. So, although unstable, the journalistic field continues to operate according to its own doxa.

Having outlined field theory, the following two sections demonstrate what kind of discourse relating to technology has emerged and constituted a piece of doxa in the journalistic field, and how individual journalists are configured within the field with regards to the discourse articulated broadly in the industry. Survey as well as trade magazine content analysis will illustrate the values that surround journalistic work and journalists' professional relationship to technology.

What They Talk About When They Talk About Technology

It is important to understand how the journalism industry as a whole thinks about technology. This is because journalistic doxa and cultural capital are discursively formed.[24] Journalists have discursively negotiated and established their own legitimacy as a way to tap into society's broader legitimizing process.[25] For example, as Tim Vos and Gregory Perreault explain, journalists have defined their legitimacy in terms of their contribution to democracy, modernity, and scientific thinking: legitimacy is expressed through such discourse as being a "watchdog of the public interest" or promoting the idea that "democracy dies in darkness."[26] Likewise, the use of technology can be legitimized through discourse. And the broad institutional discourse concerning technology will have an impact on how journalists think about and understand technology. This section analyzes the larger discourse of the journalistic field about technology.

The *New York Times Innovation* report, mentioned at the beginning of this chapter, is an example of such institutional discourse. The report prescribed a drastic overhaul of its newsroom. The ninety-six-page document called for a more business-oriented newsroom and the development of young, technologically savvy reporters. For the promotion of digital business, it argued, the traditional separation between the editorial and marketing departments needed to be broken down: the very first step to improve reader experience should be "a deliberate push to abandon our current metaphors of choice—'the wall' and 'church and state.'"[27] Specifically, it suggested, "At *The Times*, discovery, promotion and engagement have been pushed to the margins, typically left to our business-side colleagues or handed to small teams in the newsroom. The newsroom needs to claim its seat at the table because packaging, promoting and sharing our journalism requires editorial oversight."[28] Innovation would also link business and news through "product managers," whose job would be introducing ideas for new products, according to the report. Another axis of innovation, perhaps more important, is constant innovation in technology: "Unlike a printed newspaper (which is published to near perfection and launched once a day), a digital experiment should be released quickly and refined through a cycle of continuous improvement, measuring performance, shuttering losers and building on winners."[29] The report is full of business-school jargon about "innovative disruptions" or Schumpeterian "creative destruction" and almost reads like a consulting analysis prepared by McKinsey & Company.

Innovation is not wrong. Removing the fixation with print and going "all digital" and promoting more commercial interests is probably the right direction, a much-needed step to stay relevant in the highly competitive new media landscape. And whether because of this report or not, the *New York Times* appears to be doing pretty well as it enters the 2020s. It solidified its status as an innovative digital news company. However, nowhere in the report can one find a discussion on what it means for journalism and how the paper can maintain (or regain) the readers' trust. Instead, it is all about competition and survival, and toward that end it recommends relentless technological innovations, barely specifying what such innovations would entail.

The *New York Times*, as a leader in both US and global media, plays a key role in the societal discourse of the United States and the media industry overall. It sets the agenda of the industry. Likewise, the company's own discourse about its internal operations, shown in the *Innovation* report, reveals a lot about what the leaders in journalism think about their industry and their future. It is an example of journalism's institutional discourse, also known as metajournalism. Metajournalistic discourse, usually expressed through journalism trade publications and conferences, is the site in which journalistic actors engage in processes of establishing definitions, setting boundaries, and rendering judgments about journalism's legitimacy in society.[30] Analysis of metadiscourse may reveal important insights about journalism and technology because it can highlight the kinds of innovation news organizations to which should aspire.[31] Several scholars thus have studied discourses in journalism trade publications to gain a better understanding of the industry's internal beliefs and orientations.[32] Following this tradition, I analyzed more recent metajournalistic discourse on technological innovations to understand how the actors in the journalistic field talk about technology and innovation.

One particular study that informed my metajournalistic discourse analysis was Matt Powers's work on how technologically specific work is discussed in journalism. Powers analyzed journalism trade publications between 1975 and 2011 to find out the ways that journalists argue among themselves about the role technology plays in their work. He found three broad discursive themes: journalists see (1) *technological change as inevitable* and proceed to discuss technologically specific work on the grounds of how technologies can be used to ensure the continued existence of dominant practices and values; (2) *technologies as threats* to be subordinated because new forms are seen as representing practices and values that differ from commonly held journalistic standards; and (3) *technologies as journalistic reinvention* due to the capacity of new forms to transform existing journalistic values in the future.[33] In my own metajournalistic discourse analysis of more recent technologies, similar themes emerged. I label them as follows: (1) technology as a means to reinvent and save journalism; (2) technology as inevitably continuing or enhancing dominant journalistic practices; and (3) technology as a force to be cautioned against and feared.

Following Powers and other journalistic metadiscourse analysis scholars, I analyzed articles from the following leading industry publications between 2005 and mid-2020: *Editor and Publisher, Nieman Lab, Broadcasting and Cable, American Journalism Review*, and *Columbia Journalism Review*.[34] The year 2005 was chosen as a starting point because it was around this time that the so-called web 2.0 technologies and other interesting technological innovations were starting to flourish, producing rich discussion about the relationship between journalism and technology within the industry. I searched these publications' databases, using the terms "technology" and "innovation" as well as more technology-specific terms like "virtual/ augmented reality," "artificial intelligence," "blockchain," "programming/ coding," "data journalism," "social media," and so on, which yielded several hundred articles. From this initial sample, I focused on editorials and opinion pieces, thereby making the final sample size 196. Following the principles of a grounded theory analysis method, I read through the articles, making notes about how they considered various concepts.[35] In grounded theory, data exploration and theory building occur at the same time. It is an inductive process in which the researcher attempts to not only conceptualize the data but also to explore connections among conceptual categories to specify the conditions under which theoretical relationships may manifest.[36] After my initial reading, I then reread the articles more closely, looking for emerging themes and patterns. I later returned to the articles one last time and wrote notes concerning the themes. That's how the three themes—(1) reinventing and saving; (2) inevitability; and (3) caution and fear—were identified.

The most dominant theme, which made up about a half of all the articles (45 percent), was reinventing and saving journalism through technology. In this mode of discourse, new technologies were talked about as the basis for journalistic reinvention because of their transformative capacities that could help save the faltering business. Much like the theme of reinvention identified in Powers's study, technology is considered to be not only contributing to existing practices and values but also transforming them in an uncertain future by creating wholly novel types of journalism.[37] The articles in this mode showed the sentiment of excitement and optimism about technology. These are some of the headlines that capture such attitudes: "The Future Is Now"; "Paradigm Shift"; "Break New Ground"; "Time to Swing for the Fences"; "Big Game Changer"; "The Innovation Arsenal." More specifically, a 2012 *Editor and Publisher* piece urged newsrooms to buy into big data's future with a rather romanticized tone, saying, "Perhaps someone tinkering in an IBM lab or a dorm room filled with discarded Red Bull cans will come up with the way to turn the growing stores of data into gold."[38] Similarly, asking news businesses to explore business opportunities for "connected cars," another *Editor and Publisher* article in 2015 claimed that by 2020, 90 percent of cars will have online capabilities and that connected cars would bring in $152 billion, which, at this time of writing, didn't happen at all.[39] Another example of how technology—in this case, artificial intelligence—is transforming journalism can be found in a 2016 *Columbia Journalism Review* piece, where the author argued, "Quietly and without the fanfare of their robot cousins, the cyborgs are coming to journalism. And they're going to win because they can do things that neither people nor programs can do alone."[40]

The excitement about new technologies also came with the feeling of urgency that journalists and news organizations must innovate to survive. The articles often lamented the conservative nature of newsrooms and urged them to innovate quickly and adopt new things—or else they would die. For example, in a 2008 *American Journalism Review* piece titled "Maybe It Is Time to Panic," the author argued that newspapers should both make acceptable profits and perform essential public services "by moving far faster than conventional media are moving now, accelerating into a space-race urgency to revolutionize their content and business."[41]

Overall, the theme of reinventing and saving journalism through technology is well captured in these two editorials published in the New Year's issues of *Broadcasting and Cable* in 2011 and 2012, respectively.

In technology, we can't wait to see what the next iPad is, and how media companies will keep leveraging these new toys to stay ahead of the constantly changing curve. . . . Overall, there is much to be optimistic about. The quickly evolving content delivery world is mandating that we adapt and invent business models swiftly. That pressure is forcing the media world to be at the top of its game. We are seeing a level and speed of innovation that is unrivaled in recent times. Frankly, that's the media industry we love to cover.[42]

So, come out of the corner swinging this year. Take big risks. Make big plays. Don't forget where you came from, but don't be afraid to go to new places. Pump up those profits through greatness and innovation, not by cutting back and hiding. If you do all of that, no matter what happens elsewhere, you'll give yourself the best chance of excellence in 2012. And we'll be pulling for you.[43]

The second prevalent theme, which comprised about 35 percent of the sample, was technology as inevitability. What makes this theme different from the theme of reinventing and saving was that technology is seen as a way to attain and enhance traditional journalistic objectives and practices, rather than something that breaks them. Technology in this theme is regarded as "ensuring the continued, sometimes even strengthened, existence of dominant occupational practices and values."[44] In other words, the discourse acknowledges that technology is an inevitable force in journalism and seeks how technology can be better utilized for the continuation of journalistic work. For example, an *Editor and Publisher* story, in discussing artificial intelligence, maintained a moderate tone, saying, "AI is not about replacing reporting or editing. It will make journalists better at all the things they already do and serve readers with the news they want in more personal ways and on a far vaster number of topics."[45] Similarly, another *Editor and Publisher* story in 2018 adopted a cautiously optimistic view of the augmented reality technology, saying that it had become "a fluid part of *The New York Times* articles and doesn't detract from the reading flow of the story" without overly complicated production each time.[46] Overall, in this mode of the discourse, the articles emphasized that newsrooms should prepare for and adapt to new technologies to enhance their work and increase their journalistic values.

The third theme, which was the least frequent, at about 20 percent, involved critique of technologies as well as expressions of fear and caution. Here, the articles expressed a concern that technologies present threats that challenge journalism's core norms and central occupational practices. For example, quite differently from other *Editor and Publisher* articles espousing AI, a 2018 piece in the magazine, titled "An Editor Is Not an Algorithm," argued, "An editor uses experience, skepticism, instinct and insight to report valuable information. People will be willing to pay for that. Artificial intelligence is no match for solid journalism."[47] Similarly, a *Nieman Lab* blog post said, "Long championed as a transformational force that will disrupt everything, artificial intelligence has most consistently disrupted hypers and not much else."[48] This caution and critique against technology often came with a discussion of what journalism's values are and what journalists should do: "There's a good reason journalists are so wary of innovation. Daring new experiments intended to save newspapers must not destroy their souls. They must not turn print journalists into spinning tops, whirling from podcasts to vodcasts to radio appearances to online chats to blogging, then clutching their video cameras as they rush to an assignment and, if they get a free second, trying to squeeze in a little reporting."[49]

Taken together, about 80 percent of the articles belonged to either the "reinventing and saving" or "inevitability" theme. Therefore, what this meta-journalistic discourse analysis suggests is that when insiders talk about journalism and technology, they talk as if technology is a decisively powerful force that may make or break the industry's fate.

One may not discount the power of such discourse as just "talk." Discourse has real power to shape the contours of the journalistic field. It helps orient action in the world itself. As Michael Schudson argues, journalistic practices take on a normative character through discursive articulation.[50] For example, years of discussion and debate about the value of transparency in journalism eventually became an important part of contemporary journalism doxa, as represented in the ethics of the Society of Professional Journalists.[51] Likewise, the technology discourse may have tangible power in the field, as is apparent in journalism education. In addition to offering coursework in more traditional skills, such as interviewing and writing, college journalism departments are under pressure to innovate, such as by adding courses in data journalism, coding, and web development. Some of the top journalism programs in the United States have even launched joint degree programs in journalism and computer science. As Powers argues, technology-infused programs springing up at journalism schools throughout the United States over the past several years do not arise due merely to some objective necessity for technological talent, but rather as a reflection of the ascendancy of the "reinvention" discourse.[52] The call by industry leaders and news professionals to reinvent journalism programs in order to better prepare students for the technological demands of today's jobs must have had an impact on the revamped journalism curricula.[53] Technology is legitimized as a vital part of journalism education through discourse.

Imagine a competent journalist of today and the near future. One of the increasingly common images involves a tech-savvy reporter who scrapes data from the web, someone who codes and programs and masterfully weaves the data into a compelling multimedia narrative. Or maybe it is someone who stores important data in the immutable blockchain and securely communicates with her sources. Just take a look at the latest job postings in journalism; they are full of ads seeking "data journalists," "story engineers," "digital entrepreneurs," and "visual storytellers," all of which require advanced computer and digital technology skills. Here is one recent job ad for an entry-level video journalist for NBC News:

> We are seeking a news junkie to craft analysis about the day's headlines circulating around the US, as well as contribute to features and documentaries in new and imaginative ways that engage viewers through social and on mobiles. You should excel at scripting or writing tight copy, and though it won't always be required, be capable of shooting and editing your own pieces. You should be able to approach your reporting in a fun, fresh and even comedic manner when necessary but have the ability to pivot back to your traditional journalistic sensibilities as well. Most importantly, we want you to be as ecstatic as we are about building a new product under the NBC name.
>
> Basic qualifications include at least 3+ years of work experience, strong scriptwriting skills, strong working knowledge of Final Cut Pro or Adobe Premiere and Photoshop, experience in field and studio production, ideally creating pieces that range from political analysis to investigative features, CMS experience and basic understanding of HTML, CSS and JavaScript, and someone who is an experienced DSLR shooter. A bilingual in English and Spanish is a plus.[54]

This ad asks a lot for a junior position that will probably pay at most $50,000 a year. It requires a young reporter to excel in every aspect of news production, along with a high degree of multifaceted technology skills. This is the portrait of a competent journalist today: someone who is technologically adept, a jack-of-all-trades in digital technologies, who can work across multiple platforms; someone who possesses entrepreneurship and can navigate the ever-changing technological environment; someone who is a specialist in a certain topic or modality but, at the same time, a generalist capable of doing everything from copyediting to web designing.

Once reporters are hired, they then must perpetually keep up with the latest technologies and rapid market changes because news organizations are always experimenting with new tools and technologies. And it is expected that the reporters must learn the new tools and skills on their own time and dime because many news organizations do not have enough resources or simply care little about the development of individual journalists. This constant pressure on individual journalists can be stressful and damaging. That was the sentiment found in my survey of journalists' attitudes toward both technology and the news organizations they work for. Along with my colleague Kate Fink, in the second half of 2020 we surveyed 226 journalists employed in major news organizations in the United States. The journalists were randomly sampled from Investigative Reporters and Editors, a premier US journalistic occupational group.[55] According to the survey, the vast majority (74 percent) of the journalists believed digital tools and technologies, such as web design and development, coding, multimedia, and artificial intelligence, are either "very" or "extremely" important in their work, and about 40 percent of them said they feel at least some pressure from their peers to catch up with these technologies. However, only a small percentage of them use those technologies in their work, on at least a weekly basis, as table 1 suggests. Their chief motivations to use the technologies are twofold. First, many of them believe the tools help them produce better content by making their news work influential, faster, easier, credible, and more approachable to the audience. Second, they believe these technologies help

Table 1 Frequency of technology use (%)

	Never	Monthly	Biweekly	Weekly	Daily
Data visualization tools	53.4	21.3	6.2	10.7	8.4
Databases (e.g., SQL)	48.0	21.3	7.6	10.2	12.9
Programming	66.3	13.3	1.3	5.8	13.3
Web design and development	37.1	9.4	4.9	9.8	38.8
Video/audio production and editing	40.0	16.4	4.0	9.8	29.8
Artificial intelligence	80.4	6.7	1.3	6.7	4.9
Virtual/augmented reality	95.5	4.5	0	0	0

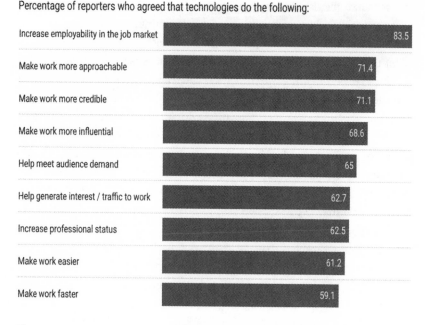

Percentage of reporters who agreed that technologies do the following:

Increase employability in the job market	83.5
Make work more approachable	71.4
Make work more credible	71.1
Make work more influential	68.6
Help meet audience demand	65
Help generate interest / traffic to work	62.7
Increase professional status	62.5
Make work easier	61.2
Make work faster	59.1

Chart 2 Journalists' motivations for technology use

enhance their professional status and career. In particular, they strongly believe that possessing technological skills would enhance their employability in the journalistic job market, as shown in chart 2.

These results present the journalists' somewhat complex and conflicting attitudes toward the latest technologies: the respondents think digital tools are important overall and recognize the necessity to learn and use some of them, but not too many actually use them on a consistent basis. This may have been the case because what journalists hear and see a lot today is the importance and power of technology—the discourse of technology shown in the previous section—but their actual practice does not necessarily require an advanced use of technology. In other words, journalists feel more pressure than needed because the dominant discourse in the industry emphasizes technology adoption and utilization as a silver bullet. As one mid-career reporter in Los Angeles said, "If we are to survive, journalism organizations need to become technology organizations. I feel like I am behind. I did not learn data visualization, coding, web design, and data tools, but I know all of those tools are a big part of the future of storytelling."

While they talk about innovation and technology all the time, the reality and bottom line often fall way short and do not match the rhetoric. The respondents find little time and few resources to learn and keep up with the technologies. As a New York–based reporter said, "I would love to be able to use innovation and technology. However, our resources are very small, and we are struggling to keep going. I have to work about fifteen hours a day, seven days [a week], in order to keep running, with not enough time to learn more about technology." An independent reporter from Oregon voiced a similar concern: "My biggest challenge is fighting for time to stay current with the tech skills I've developed because there is a constant demand for news, and quick stories fill that need more immediately than in-depth and thought-out data-driven reporting."

The reporters surveyed consistently pointed out the lack of training and support from their organizations. In many newsrooms, the task of using and keeping up with the latest technologies is left to individual journalists. This remark from a newspaper reporter from New Orleans sums up the current state of technology training: "[We get] less than sparse training in using technology. At best, we were told of a new tool and expected to learn how to use it on our own with no direction, training, et cetera. At worst, we were not even told about a new tool, [we] just had to discover and learn it on our own."

Almost all open-ended answers from reporters belonging to news outlets other than the *New York Times* and *USA Today* lamented the fact that they must catch up with new tools while the everyday demand for work is already onerous and their organizations provide little to no support. This tendency illustrates an important point that has been going on in the industry for a while: journalism institutions' neoliberalization puts burdens on individuals in the name of individual liberty and responsibility. The neoliberal project consists of economic deregulation, privatization, and unfettered competition in the global market. In such a framework, management attempts to cut costs by requiring journalists to take on labor previously performed by relatively expensive technical specialists, or by relieving journalists of work tasks that can be done by relatively inexpensive workers instead.[56] Furthermore, the latest technological tools are utilized to extract greater productivity at minimal management cost and worker resistance. As Caitlin Petre, who has studied modern use of analytic technology, aptly observes, "the newsroom analytics dashboard, like the stopwatch, is a technological artifact that extracts increased productivity from workers—but it does so in a way that obfuscates, rather than highlights, managerial influence in the newsroom."[57] This strong neoliberal ideology makes management believe that individual journalists are malleable enough to fit into ever-changing models of news production, which reveals a workplace structure that is contingent on each individual's ability to recognize and readily incorporate shifting conditions into their work routines.[58]

Journalistic institutions today regard technologies as a vital force to save the struggling industry, and yet the deployment and utilization of them are largely left to individuals. Worse, the failure to produce profitable news products from those technologies may be blamed on individual journalists. Within this neoliberal framework, "overt discourses of individual freedom and responsibility alongside specific policies that define institutional failure as the result of an individual's deficiency further obscure the ways in which public institutions fail to meet their normative ideals at a structural level."[59] As this happens, journalists increasingly experience workplace burnouts, stress, and fatigue, which was shared by many reporters surveyed. The technological-organizational pressure makes them wonder what the meaning of their work is, and ultimately what journalism is. A broadcast reporter in Washington, DC, said, "Tool fatigue is real. . . . I spend a lot of time on planning and workflow, and it is frustrating to me that many tools do not allow more third-party integration so that we can reduce the number of interfaces that the team must use (it's 2 p.m. on a Monday, and I have already used conference calls, Teams, WhatsApp, Asana, Slack, and email . . . all for work). I bring this up because reducing tool fatigue will allow our journalists the time and space to focus on what matters: diverse source development, deeper reporting, listening to the audience." Another broadcast reporter in the Northeast was frustrated with her newsroom's requirements for social media activity, which may hurt the actual journalistic endeavor she finds important:

> I have Facebook and Twitter quotas (three posts and ten tweets, respectively). While I value engaging on social media, I worry that this takes time and energy away from the actual work. I can spend all day getting an exclusive interview with a reluctant source, digging through court documents, and putting together a story for the 6 p.m. broadcast. But if I only post two times on Facebook that day, it's an issue. And a selfie or picture of my dog will generate more "likes" than a story explaining a new bill in the state house. . . . When my value is based more on being a personality than on my

experience as a reporter, where do I go? How can newsrooms stay current but also stay healthy when it comes to social media and digital tools? Audiences sense when something is authentic. I'm worried that quotas and chasing engagement numbers are hurting us.

With an emphasis on functional technical skills and quick fixes to increase traffic to news products, it becomes increasingly difficult for journalists to hone the traditional craft of journalism, such as good interviewing skills, source development and networking, understanding context, verification and fact-checking, and good writing. Some scholars thus argue that in today's technology-focused journalism, deskilling or reskilling of journalists is taking place. For example, in a study of British and Spanish journalists, José Alberto García Avilés and colleagues found the fact that technology allowing for faster processing of news increases the pressure to be first with the story and to provide more on-the-spot, instantaneous live news, which leaves very little chance to explain context.[60] Likewise, it was shown that Taiwanese reporters had experienced an increase in workload and an intensification of managerial control due to the introduction of new technologies in the newsroom, which resulted in a trivialization of reporting tasks and devaluation of reporters' experience and knowledge.[61] In the current survey, many reporters aired similar concerns. As more and more of their time is taken up dealing with technology, they complain that a sizable chunk of their typical day is spent solving technical issues. These journalists believed the true craft of journalism comes from traditional skills rather than digital technological competencies. As chart 3 clearly illustrates, they believe traditional skills and abilities are much more important to perform their job as a journalist.[62] These traditional skills are fundamental and seldom change, but digital skills may be more fleeting. As this seasoned AP reporter said:

> I still find that the "old school" tools of journalism, like calling sources, going to interviews, going to press conferences, and writing eloquently, are the tools that I use on a daily basis. I would like to learn how to do more with data but often don't know how it's useful in my particular stories. And I feel like I lack the basic fundamentals to understand data journalism and the language that's used. How to do Excel, for example? These are things that I use so infrequently that if I take a class on how to do it, by the time I want to use it in the field, I've forgotten everything.

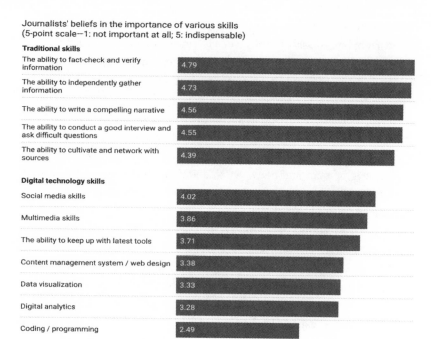

Journalists' beliefs in the importance of various skills
(5-point scale—1: not important at all; 5: indispensable)

Traditional skills

The ability to fact-check and verify information	4.79
The ability to independently gather information	4.73
The ability to write a compelling narrative	4.56
The ability to conduct a good interview and ask difficult questions	4.55
The ability to cultivate and network with sources	4.39

Digital technology skills

Social media skills	4.02
Multimedia skills	3.86
The ability to keep up with latest tools	3.71
Content management system / web design	3.38
Data visualization	3.33
Digital analytics	3.28
Coding / programming	2.49

Chart 3 Journalists' opinions of different skill sets

Again, these responses may reflect a recognition among journalists of the gap between the industry's technological aspirations and their own inability to achieve them, due to limitations on time, finances, and organizational support. But the preference for traditional skills over technological skills may also reflect a skepticism among journalists of the potential for technology to be a savior for their industry. "I'm all for new tools and new ways to tell stories," one respondent said. "But journalism is journalism. Let reporting guide the tools, not vice versa."

What are the essential skills and craft fundamental to journalism? Barbie Zelizer argues that the qualities that have constituted good journalism from its inception have been "curiosity, independence, a sense of adventure and enterprise, serendipity, exploration, creativity, resourcefulness, a flair for writing."[63] A too strong technological focus over fundamental qualities of journalism coupled with constant pressure for change and adaptation may result in journalist burnout and deterioration of their craft.

Overall, these survey results illustrate the inherent tension between the journalistic field's abiding doxa and individuals' habitus, as Bourdieu's field theory suggests. That is, the journalism doxa has become increasingly technology-deterministic in recent years, whereas individual journalists' actual practices and routines remain somewhat unchanged. It is telling that while the majority of the surveyed agonize over their lack of technological skills or seek more, there is not actually much advanced technical expertise expected of these journalists in their jobs. In fact, most newsrooms' limited workplace settings and traditional routines make it difficult for the journalists to follow the technology mandate. Their individual backgrounds, educations, and belief systems are also more aligned with traditional journalistic skills than with new technology skills. Therefore, journalists today live by the grand discourse of technology, struggling to keep up with the new tools and innovations and, at the same time, experiencing dissonance arising from their actual habitus of newswork.

The Crumbling Boundaries of the Journalistic Field

The previous sections showed the tensions that exist among various actors within the journalistic field. Even with strong internal conflicts, a field may continue to operate well, as long as the actors hold on to the field's larger normative structure. However, field theory suggests that forces outside a field—pressures coming from neighboring fields—present more serious challenges. Looking at the neighbors of the journalistic field, that's exactly what's happening these days. From politics to technology to citizen journalism, strong outside forces are threatening the professional boundaries of the journalistic field. Journalism is a very permeable occupation, and its boundaries are now being blurred, renegotiated, and redefined from the influence of many different social fields. Traditionally, it has been the political and economic fields that have exercised strong influences on the journalistic field through such measures as media regulations and commercial logics, although the journalistic field has reciprocated, too. In addition to politics and the economy, now the journalistic field faces threats from the scientific and medicinal fields, whose actors engage in journalism as well. In the broader field of civil society, nongovernmental organizations like Human Rights Watch provide lively and vital news reports from the ground, often with a tone of advocacy, reshaping the journalistic boundary.[64] As I documented in my previous work, what is known as citizen journalism and its participatory ideology is a powerful force that makes the professional journalistic field even more porous.[65]

It is worth mentioning that two neighboring social fields played particularly important roles with regard to the journalistic field's tighter association with technology in recent years: those of philanthropy and technology. First, the philanthropy field is a powerful sphere that has shaped journalism's forms, missions, and identities. Especially in the United States, foundations, think tanks, and philanthropic organizations occupy an ex officio space in the public life, exercising a formidable influence on public discourse and driving social changes behind the scenes.[66] For example, behind the public journalism movement of the 1990s, which conceived of journalists as active participants in community life rather than detached spectators, was the Pew Charitable Trusts, which set the agenda of the journalistic reform movement. As the former *St. Louis Post-Dispatch* editor William Woo once acknowledged, it is safe to say that without Pew, public journalism would not have achieved a fraction of the impact it has had.[67]

Another influential actor in the field is the Knight Foundation, founded by the Knight family, originators of Knight Ridder, one of the largest media companies in the United States during the twentieth century. The foundation supported movements like public journalism, and, since 2006, it has conducted the Knight News Challenge, a contest that seeks to fund innovative ideas that develop platforms, tools, and services to inform and transform community news, conversations, and information distribution using digital media. Seth Lewis's study of the Knight News Challenge suggests that the initiative opened up journalism—its definition and the boundaries around its practice—to a wider set of fields, especially technologists.[68] Because it was open to non-journalists as well as professionals, and because of the acclaim and impact its winners have generated, the Knight News Challenge assumed an outsized role in setting the agenda for news innovation. In doing so, the Knight Foundation "has emerged as a boundary-spanning agent, expanding its influence within journalism and beyond."[69] In fact, many of the Challenge winners come from nontraditional journalism, such as digital games, databases, wikis, and other technology projects.

The Knight Foundation's focus on technology and the development of viable news business models through the News Challenge differs from its previous emphasis on "informed and engaged communities" as a bedrock value of journalistic innovation. According to Brian Creech and Anthony Nadler, who conducted a discourse analysis of the Knight Foundation's documents, the organization's conceptualization of journalistic innovation has changed from a community-centered value to more elite-centered notions of news quality, technological sophistication, and revenue sustainability. They show that the foundation assesses the success of a journalism project by measuring how their funding has supported leaders in the news field and sites credited with producing high-quality news, rather than by measuring the impact of individual projects on communities.[70] As such, the Knight Foundation and its initiatives have been instrumental in promoting a more business-technology-oriented conceptualization of journalistic innovation and has altered the boundaries of journalism's jurisdiction.

Second, the larger technological field's influence on and interaction with the journalistic field warrants closer examination. The technology field here refers to a social sphere comprising technology companies and their products, technology think tanks and policies, individual engineers and computer scientists, and so on. Internally, the journalistic field has been able to take in and grow technology personnel conforming to the norms of the journalistic profession, as noted above. However, powerful technology firms exist outside the journalistic field, with their own doxa. These bodies and their technologies were developed not specifically for journalism, and, therefore, carry with them assumptions, goals, and rules that might not be consistent with journalism's internal standards.[71] And the weakly autonomous journalistic field becomes increasingly susceptible to the ever-powerful technology field. One prime example is the case of *Upworthy*. Since its founding in 2012, the site, which circulated viral news content exclusively through Facebook, had been regarded as one of the fastest-growing media properties ever.[72] At its peak, almost ninety million people a month visited the site, an enviable number for most news organizations. But after Facebook altered its algorithms a couple of times, its visitors plummeted to about twenty million in 2014.[73] By 2017, it was acquired by another company, and many of its staffers were let go. Today, few remember or use the media platform. The story of *Upworthy* is one where a once-promising journalistic actor was mercilessly subjected to the rules of the powerful technological field. This struggle of the journalistic field against the technology field is also observed in empirical studies. For example, because of Google's search-ranking algorithms, journalists who wanted their news articles to be easily findable had to adjust their headline writing styles based on the tenets of search engine optimization.[74] Similarly, when Facebook tweaked its news feed algorithms in 2014 to prioritize native videos, it did not just change its own internal rules but also imposed them on users, including news organizations traditionally governed by the journalistic field's own norms.[75] After all, many news organizations had to play by the social media giant's rules so as not to lose its audience.

This threat of the technological field taking over journalism is one reason news organizations are keen on the idea of their own technological innovation. Against the powerful external threat, the actors within the journalistic field attempt to increase their technological capital and preserve their autonomy. They do not want to follow the path of publications like *Upworthy*, at the mercy of technology giants. It would be difficult for news organizations today to completely separate themselves from the tech giants' platforms because that's where the audience and money lie, but they realize that a key to their survival is diversifying revenue streams, both with and without the tech giants.[76] In addition to utilizing tech platforms to reach audiences, news organizations are now engaged in developing their own technological products and competencies. News organizations used to depend on third-party technological tools and platforms for data science, visualization, and audience research, but they are increasingly developing their own tech products and incorporating them into their external and internal operations.[77] Much like true technology companies, the *New York Times*, the *Wall Street Journal*, and the *Washington Post* operate research and development labs where they incorporate everything from machine learning to spatial computing and comment moderation. Poaching technologists from tech companies is increasingly a common occurrence. The new CEO of the New York Times Company even declared that the legacy paper will be a "tech company."[78]

The technology field's influence on journalism comes from other directions as well, molding it to be further receptive to the idea of technological innovation. Over the last several years, companies like Google and Facebook made conscious efforts to be directly involved in journalism by setting up funds, fellowships, and training programs. The Google News Initiative and Facebook's Journalism Project are prime examples. The Google News Initiative has provided a huge amount of money to news organizations worldwide with few stipulations. Not only that, but it maintains extensive fellowship and training programs for journalists and collaborates amicably with such main players in the journalistic field as the Society of Professional Journalists, Columbia University's Journalism School, and the Reuters Institute for the Study of Journalism at Oxford University. It also sponsors technology-journalism conferences worldwide and offers a vast array of technological tools to journalists and news organizations. Google News Lab, in particular, provides attractive opportunities to practicing journalists. Facebook's foray into the journalistic field came slightly later than Google's, but it is rapidly expanding its programs, hoping to bring news organizations together for innovation. In true philanthropic fashion, Google and Facebook in 2020 even provided "emergency relief funds" to news organizations suffering from the fallouts of the COVID-19 pandemic.

But Google and Facebook are, after all, not philanthropic organizations. Their journalism projects are aimed at safeguarding their long-term business interests. The Google News Initiative's €150 million funding program can be seen as an attempt to win over the publishers as well as the regulators and the public, who have often criticized the search giant for monopolizing the European information sphere. Likewise, promoting Google tools in their journalist education programs not only ensures Google's continued business success but also helps develop journalists' affinity for the company, which may turn out to be an important asset in the long term. Facebook seems to have the same goal in mind. The social media giant has been heavily criticized for proliferating fake news, misinformation, and extreme hate speech, and many journalists and members of the public are disenchanted with the once-hip company. Promoting such programs as local news fellowships are a much-needed move to turn around its negative public image. Facebook's Journalism Project also doesn't forget to promote its business interest. For example, its education program, titled "Mastering Facebook Live for News," is an obvious attempt to make journalists use their products more.

Through grants, education, and fellowship programs, the tech giants have forayed into the journalistic field in order to tame its actors. They shape journalism's forms, agenda, and even its missions and functions in society. No specific datasets exist on how the companies' money was used for newsrooms in the United States, but research from the European Journalism Observatory provides useful insights about the controlling power of Google.[79] The research found that more than half of the funding since 2015 has been given to traditional commercial publishing houses and that the vast majority of them were based in Western Europe; only 10 percent of the projects went to nonprofit or public service media. Furthermore, about 40 percent of the projects funded were about data journalism and automation, the area where Google has the strongest expertise and business interests. The study concludes that the Google News Initiative in Europe promoted a certain business model tied to technology. This way, Google shapes the contours of the journalistic field. Actors in the journalistic field follow Google's lead, which helps drive the newsrooms' pursuit of technological innovation.

Because these companies at their core are all about generating profits through software and hardware engineering, journalism is not their main concern. Emily Bell, director of the Tow Center for Digital Journalism, met with many news people who work for Facebook and Google and says that journalistic work in those companies, if any, is relegated to marginal departments. As she sharply points out, "Miles away from the ritzy conferences like Newsgeist and the meetings for Facebook Journalism Project, in the central loci of technology businesses, executives generally don't care that much about journalism. They see it as the Pluto in their solar system—a part of what they do but rather small and very far away. They care about journalism in the same way I care about clean water and aircraft safety—deeply and often—but this does not qualify me to be involved in its development."[80]

It is the journalistic field that makes a fuss about what technology companies do to journalism. On the contrary, the Facebooks and Googles of the world don't care much about what journalism does. They care about journalism mostly when it serves their business interests. It is like an unreciprocated, exploitative love relationship. For that reason, journalism should break away and operate on its own. How does it do that? By focusing on its core mission and identity, which is the subject of this book's final chapter and conclusion.

This chapter documented the attitudes of reporters as well as the journalism industry's institutional discourse, demonstrating the presence of a strong technological narrative within the field. Many journalists surveyed regarded technology and technological development as inevitable and powerful forces in their work, which is consistent with the findings from other studies.[81] At the same time, these journalists are under constant pressure to catch up with the newest developments in technologies, which resulted in a high level of stress and a potential devaluation of essential journalistic skills, such as networking, source development, and fact-checking. This troublesome understanding of technology by individual journalists can be viewed as being influenced by the larger discourse in the journalistic field. As the analysis has shown, the dominant discourse in the field is that of technological determinism, such that technology is viewed as a savior that can reinvent journalism and rescue it from the current perils. This institutional discourse has real power in shaping the direction of the journalistic field, and it brings about the notion of technologically adept journalists who create innovative content and routines, managing journalism's crisis themselves.[82]

A technological narrative in journalism has been present probably since the invention of the printing press and the birth of newspapers. But its magnitude and impact are more strongly felt in our late modern capitalistic society. As Henrik Örnebring and other scholars suggest, technology today plays the role of a servant of capitalism rather than a force itself: technology has become a tool that allows managers to implement business and organizational strategies to make journalistic labor more efficient and more easily controlled.[83] Add to this the fact that the journalistic field is increasingly becoming unstable and faces threats from other fields, such as technology and politics, and it is more and more likely to resort to the mythical power of technology as a savior of the field.

Journalism, Going Slow

There is more to life than increasing its speed.

—Mahatma Gandhi

Technologies are important in journalism. They change the nature of news-work and sometimes even journalists themselves. They create new markets and revenue and alter audience behavior. Although I argued in chapter 1 that the impact of various technologies on journalism has been gradual and moderated by many different sociocultural factors, technologies like the computer and the internet in the end dramatically changed the way news is produced and consumed—the fate of some newsrooms was heavily influenced by the technologies they adopted. That's why the discourse of journalistic innovation is full of technological adoption and use, as the previous chapter revealed. To survive, to generate profits, and to maintain its occupational boundaries and relevance, the journalistic field is in search of constant technological innovation.

This is a rather recent phenomenon. Media organizations, especially newspapers, used to be known for their traditionalism and conservative attitudes toward change. They used to get labeled as Luddites, or anti-technologists, for denying new technological adoption.[1] But things have changed quickly, especially after the internet revolution in the mid to late 1990s. Many saw fellow journalists and rival newsrooms swept away by technological forces; some, fortunately, experienced breakthroughs thanks to smart moves. Maybe that's why news organizations today are keen on technological innovation—the scar of failure and the memory of turmoil, disruption, and breakthroughs during the early days of the internet and social media revolutions are still fresh. In addition, the economic pressure and threats from technology giants are greater now than ever, compelling many news organizations to follow the business adage "the only constant is change." Under the fear that they will lag behind and become irrelevant, news organizations are engaged in heightened efforts at technological innovation.

But the contemporary pursuit of technology is hectic and haphazard. There were newsrooms that bought dozens of Google Glasses, believing the new gadget would drastically change how journalism is conducted, yet the devices are hard to find these days; not too long ago, "chatbots," or conversational artificial intelligence agents, were all the rage, and news organizations invested quickly to deploy them, though few today are still in use; the VR/AR project is not taking off, and now many are trying to get in on the blockchain experiment. It is like they are throwing everything at the wall to see what sticks.

Technological innovation without careful research and planning may backfire, wasting time and resources and causing innovation fatigue. The journalistic field needs to slow down and think about what technological innovation means. This is where the idea of "slow" becomes useful. The slow movement represents a cultural shift toward slowing down life's pace, whether it is living, eating, or consuming. Applied to journalism, it means a respite from the hectic pace of newswork and constant innovation, and the appreciation of the long-term collaboration and reflection that enhance journalism's core mission and function in society. I adopt the idea of slowness not as an argument against innovation but as a plea to research carefully the effect of the introduction of new technologies to newsrooms and their effects on newsworkers, consumers, and culture more broadly. In this view, slowness does not necessarily discourage technological innovation. On the contrary, it encourages innovation by making it more sustainable with a state of mindfulness. Technologies, although important, do not dictate newsroom innovation. Successful innovation requires a careful assessment of the complex web of innovation factors that include culture, people, and audience as well as technology. This chapter discusses how successful, albeit slow, innovation can be achieved in journalism with and beyond technology.

The Slow Movement

Over the last several years, a new kind of social movement has been gathering steam—the slow movement. It encompasses many different social spheres, and we increasingly see such ideas as slow living, slow food, slow city, slow aging, and slow media, to name a few. The slow movement is a deliberate subversion attempt against the dominance of speed in modern life. Proponents want to reclaim the notion of time to facilitate the cultivation of not only a particular self but also an ethical orientation toward other people.[2] Slow food was a pioneering force. The movement began in Italy in the late 1980s to protest fast food and to preserve traditional and regional cuisine as well as the local ecosystem. It generated the ethics of "good, clean, and fair," which states that better food is defined by a fresh and flavorsome seasonal diet that pleasures the sense and is part of local culture (good); it does not harm the environment, animal welfare, and human health (clean); and it provides accessible prices for consumers and fair conditions and pay for small-scale producers (fair).[3] These core principles have resonated beyond food to many areas of culture and daily life. For example, slow media is not about fast consumption of cheap content but about choosing the ingredients mindfully and preparing them in a concentrated manner.[4] Popular culture caught up with the slow movement when Oprah Winfrey did the "What Can You Live Without?" challenge, where she encouraged people to consume and use less—especially digital devices like tablet PCs and smartphones. In my own college, a "media fast" has become a popular assignment, in which students disconnect themselves from digital devices for a certain period of time. Students usually write about feelings of "detoxification" and "invigoration" after a media fast—if their reports are to be believed at face value.

Is the slow movement a fad? Is it some kind of new-age hipster shtick? After all, how many among the general public who struggle to make ends meet would care about slow living, slow and often costly cooking, and fair trading? And when it was popularized on such shows as *Oprah* and quickly subsided, one could not shake the feeling that it is the latest craze or gimmick. But the slow movement is not just a romantic escape from hectic daily life, nor is it a superficial experience of a spiritual life momentarily purchased by upper-middle-class urbanites. The movement and its values are rooted in serious philosophy. From the Buddhist concept of "mindfulness," where one tries to be aware of present thoughts, feelings, and sensations without fast judgment, to Friedrich Nietzsche, who argued for "slow reading," which is a deliberate reduction in the speed of reading to increase comprehension and pleasure, the slow movement comes out of a long tradition.[5] It also has strong connections to the American philosophy of transcendentalism of the nineteenth century, in which such figures as Ralph Waldo Emerson and Henry David Thoreau believed individuals have knowledge about themselves and the world around them that transcends what they can see; based on this belief, transcendentalists sought an "original relation to universe," which may be obtained by a slower pace in life that syncs to nature.[6] It's only because some companies and self-help gurus today use these ideas as a marketing ploy, a panacea for all the ills of modern life, that it got a less serious reputation.

The philosophical idea of slow has been manifested and further materialized since the 1970s as the sustainability movement. Jennifer Rauch, in her book *Slow Media*, explains that a paradigm shift toward the idea of sustainability took place with such events as the first celebration of Earth Day in 1970 and the 1972 United Nations Conference on the Human Environment, which urged the protection of natural resources and wildlife alongside human rights.[7] The idea became even stronger with the environmental and counterculture movement of that era in the United States and Western Europe. This "paradigm shift" offered an alternative way of life that supports economic viability and healthy ecosystems by modifying consumption patterns and implementing a more equitable social framework, which became the backbone idea of the larger slow movement today.[8]

I would also like to make an explicit connection between the slow movement and some tenets of Buddhist philosophy. The slow movement, which began in the heart of the modern West, shares a remarkable similarity with the ancient Eastern philosophy's view of time. In Buddhism, time is not an objective entity or independent reality apart from one's consciousness— time is realized in and through the realization of the impermanence of everything in the universe.[9] This is because a fundamental doctrine of Buddhism considers all conditioned things in the world to be impermanent: everything is a process; nothing can arise independently, and nothing can be the outcome of a single cause. Time in Buddhism is thus infinite, with no beginning or end. This view of time contrasts with the Judeo-Christian understanding, in which time, a creation of God, is linear and bounded with a beginning (genesis) and an end (apocalypse-catharsis).[10] The Japanese Buddhist philosopher Masao Abe explains that in Christian-Western understanding, time is an independent, objective factor, such that spring gives rise to blooming flowers. But in the Buddhist understanding of time, "flowers blooming in themselves are spring coming. Flowers blooming, birds singing, and the warm wind blowing in themselves are the time called spring. There is no spring apart from these things, and no time apart from phenomenal things."[11] In other words, there is no *time priori* in Buddhism. Instead, time and things are inseparably connected with one another. What this means is that if one is to live life meaningfully and truthfully, one must be mindful of the surroundings, not bound by immediate time. When one slows down and is aware of the moment they are in, they can better connect with life. As the Zen master Thich Nhat Hanh said, "Drink your tea slowly and reverently, as if it is the axis on which the whole earth revolves—slowly, evenly, without rushing toward the future. Live the actual moment."[12] As such, the Buddhist view of time and its call to live a conscious and mindful life may serve as another backbone philosophy of the slow movement.

While it still remains largely an alternative ideology to modern capitalism, the slow movement is not a mystic or fringe Eastern philosophy, nor a mere backlash ideology produced in reaction to high-intensity consumption culture.[13] It has grown into more than just the new counterculture and has become a fairly mainstream way of tuning into one's life. One doesn't have to be in Thoreau's *Walden* or become a meditating monk to practice slow values. Slow and fast can coexist, dialectically. The goal of slower life must be situated within the present, acknowledging modern technologies and using them with reflection.[14] In the case of town planning, for example, Sofi Ambroise explains how slow and fast can coexist to create a good life. Slowness "does not imply waiting in long traffic jams, or for trams that never come. On the contrary, and paradoxically, it means having access to qualitatively slow spaces and time by means of transport that links up any two points with the maximum speed."[15] In other words, speed in modern life is also needed to enable slowness. Fast and slow coexist in a dialectical manner.

As such, slow should not be regarded as synonymous with Luddism or anti-technology. The Luddite movement refers to the early nineteenth-century violent protest in Britain led by artisans who opposed the growing use of machines in the production process.[16] Today's slow movement is more akin to what Jennifer Rauch called "post-Luddism," or a healthy skepticism and mindful consideration of technology.[17] It is an idea that the social debate over technology should go beyond the extremes of techno-utopia versus techno-dystopia and foster a deeper, more nuanced understanding of the role that technologies play in society. Post-Luddites understand that diversity, contradiction, and complexity are essential features of social life and technology use, and they attempt to advance ecological and social sustainability based on long-term principles of stability and cooperation.[18] Simply speaking, it is a more mindful use of media and technology.

Overall, the slow movement reframes the modern world by providing an alternative to fast life. It is not a return to the good ol' days, but an attempt to live in the present in a more meaningful, sustainable, and thoughtful way.

It is a "process whereby everyday life—in all its pace and complexity, frisson and routine—is approached with care and attention."[19]

Slowness in Journalism

The idea of slow caught on in journalism circles as well. Harold Gess applied the principles of good, clean, and fair in slow food to journalism. He argues that "good" journalism does careful research about information that is relevant to a particular community; "clean" journalism would be sustainable, ethical, and not corrupt or abuse the communities in which it is practiced; and "fair" journalism would allow for advocacy journalism, make media accessible to the community, and ensure nonexploitative working conditions. Gess argues that such journalism can provide a way forward for reporting stories that are not dramatic or personality-driven, but it requires a connection to communities on a more local level and over a longer period, as in the case of climate change reporting.[20] Similarly, but with some variation, Rauch argues that good journalism offers content that's satisfying to one's intellect, emotions, and senses as well as politically engaged and connected to local cultures; clean journalism is produced in ways that protect environmental health, animal welfare, and human well-being; and fair journalism shows respect to news workers, through satisfactory pay and working conditions, as well as to its readers and the wider community.[21] From a different yet related tradition, scholars also started advocating "mindful journalism," grounded in Buddhist philosophy. The dominant, Western paradigm of journalism emphasizes finite time, individualism, objective knowledge, subordination of nature to man, and reification of such textbook news values as conflict, immediacy, proximity, and prominence. But for a Buddhist, mindful journalism exemplifies infinite time, holism, experiential knowledge, interconnectedness, harmony with nature, and flexibility of news values.[22] An important goal of mindful journalism is to produce a "journalism of healing" that helps people overcome individual and social sufferings, which resonates with the values of slow journalism.[23]

These ideas are refreshing but vague. And they can be criticized as romanticizing and idealistic. What is more common, in practice, is that slow journalism manifests itself in such genres as long-form storytelling and in-depth reporting. The British publication *Delayed Gratification* is a good example.[24] The quarterly magazine, launched specifically with the slow journalism philosophy in mind, publishes print issues that revisit the last three months with in-depth coverage. The magazine uses postal mail and print paper as a medium of slow appreciation. The Dutch publication *De Correspondent* is another example. Their news avoids the breaking news cycle and instead focuses on analysis, interpretation, and investigative reporting.[25] *De Correspondent* inspired Berlin-based *Krautreporter*, which engages in independent in-depth reporting without advertising. The motto of *Jot Down*, the Spanish slow journalism news publication, is "an ode to slow production," and it focuses on long-form narrative pieces and in-depth reporting.[26] And in the United States, the rise of such long-form digital news publishers as *Narratively*, the *Atavist*, and the *New Humanitarian* (formerly *News Deeply*) attests to the rising significance of slow and in-depth journalism. How much impact these new slow journalism ventures have had on the larger journalism universe is unclear. And some of them may eventually die out in the crowded journalism market. But the point is that we hear a rising voice that journalism should be slower and more ethical, and that we witness this voice being materialized.

One may wonder how this new and often digital long-form journalism is different from long-form pieces that can be found in such traditional publications as the *New Yorker* or the *Atlantic* or *Harper's Magazine*. In fact, they are quite similar. Although not specifically labeled as slow journalism, these traditional publishers have practiced a slow model for a long time. For example, almost every story in the *New Yorker* is a long-form feature, and it usually takes at least several months for their writers to complete a piece. One can also argue that the New Journalism practiced in the 1970s by such famed writers as Tom Wolfe, Hunter S. Thompson, and Truman Capote in the United States has a connection to today's slow journalism. The New Journalism, using literary techniques, sought subjective, long-form narratives of events in which reporters immersed themselves.

What is different in today's slow journalism is that it goes beyond journalism as a genre—it is beyond certain forms or styles. It is more about certain philosophies and attitudes about journalism. It is about what journalism should be. Hence, it is a "movement." Endorsing this view that slow journalism is a certain approach to journalism, slow journalism scholars observe that "out of practice and literature arises an image of slow journalism as a counter-movement, a corrective to a kind of journalism that gives priority to the fast spreading of news and pays far less attention to other societal functions of journalism."[27] As such, today's slow journalism is best understood as a journalism reform movement.

The problems of modern, fast-moving journalism are well known. Mainstream, commercial journalism is concerned with delivering facts to the audience in a timely and objective manner. In such a model of journalism, facts and information are valued more than informed analysis or commentaries, and the flow of information from elite to citizen is prioritized more than citizen participation in public affairs.[28] To deliver facts in a most efficient manner, mainstream journalism operates with a beat system and uses such formulas as the inverted pyramid style of writing and two-sides balancing with opposing viewpoints. This form of news represents a positivist worldview, holding that there always is verifiable truth that can be easily summarized and delivered.[29] And under today's ever-growing economic pressure, news organizations have an incentive to put journalism "on an assembly line with ever-higher speeds and ever-decreasing numbers of skilled workers."[30] Accordingly, productivity becomes the most important value, and the constant need for speed quickly becomes naturalized as a technological factor outside the control of individual journalists but under the control of capital.[31] It is exactly why the eminent sociologist Herbert Gans compared today's news organizations to mass factories. According to Gans, the routinization of news production, represented by the objectivity paradigm, is important because the news media must distribute their products more regularly and punctually than most others in the era of perpetual news cycles and competition. As a result, news organizations need predictably available raw materials that can be routinely assembled by a workforce. Efficiency is integral to creating a product cheap enough to serve the audience and advertisers but profitable enough to attract entrepreneurs and investors.[32]

The consequences of factory-produced mass journalism are the public's declining trust in news products. The quickly produced, standardized news products cannot adequately explain the web of intricacies in human affairs. Such news products are also riddled with defects because emphasis on fast production puts journalists at the risk of oversimplification and stereotyping of the events reported.[33] In its race to be the first, fast journalism may also come with errors and eventually hurt credibility, an important asset of the trade.[34] Examples are numerous. In the case of the Boston Marathon bombings in 2013, which killed three and injured hundreds of people, some news outlets, in their rush to break news, incorrectly identified suspects. Journalists from such outlets as NBC News, *Newsweek*, and *Politico* spread unverified information obtained from social media.[35] Authorities even asked the media to stop reporting on police movements in order to prevent suspects from obtaining information about the ongoing manhunt, but that didn't stop the media frenzy to identify suspects on their own—and falsely. CNN was also slammed for prematurely reporting that an arrest had been made when in fact it had not.[36] Similarly, when a US domestic right-wing extremist bombed the Oklahoma City federal building in 1995, the mainstream media jumped too quickly to a conclusion, speculating that the bombing was the work of Middle Eastern terrorists. Within hours of the bombing, most network news reports described suspects with a "Middle Eastern appearance" and "dark hair and beards" and featured comments from experts on Middle Eastern terrorism.[37] The *Wall Street Journal* called it a "Beirut-style car bombing" in the first sentence of its story, and a *CBS Evening News* report, citing an anonymous government source, said that the attack has "Middle East terrorism written all over it."[38] Media failings stemming from rushed judgments can also be found in the coverage of such events as the Newtown mass shooting, the September 11 attack, and the coronavirus pandemic. One can imagine the damage such coverage would inflict on individuals as well as the public discourse: people are wrongfully accused and tried in the court of public opinion, biases and stereotypes against certain minorities are amplified, and hate crimes may increase. It may even hurt international relations. In case of the mis-coverage of health issues, it can literally harm people's bodies. A fast and misinformed news diet hurts people and the public sphere at large.

Against this phenomenon of frenetic "McNews," the idea of slow journalism provides a valuable corrective in that it challenges the assumption that news needs to be fast, efficient, and competitive. Slow foods, cooked with fair and nutritious ingredients, are not only tasty and healthy but also gain consumers' trust with ethical preparation and processing. Why not apply the same logic to news? Small-batch, artisanal news prepared by reporters who abide by ethical standards of journalism will likely be more informative, engaging, original, and impactful for the community. All news should not be slow news, just as all foods don't have to be slowly prepared. Fast, breaking news plays important roles and should coexist with slow news. But when the dominant method of news manufacture is that of top-down, efficiency-infused mass manufacturing, the values of slowness need to be further appreciated. As Geoffrey Craig argues, slow journalism is "a means by which we can ask why contemporary journalism operates according to particular social speeds and whether journalism can also be well-served through a disjuncture between its temporality and the speed of the fields which are the object of scrutiny."[39]

Slow journalism is actually one of the latest iterations in a long line of journalism reform movements, and it bears similarities to other efforts that came before it. As noted above, the New Journalism of the 1970s, although it wasn't necessarily a movement per se, was an ingenious attempt to reconsider what good journalism means, utilizing long-form, personal, and subjective narrative styles. In the late 1980s and early 1990s, the public journalism movement followed. Public journalism sought to invigorate public life through journalists' becoming more "involved" in the reporting of community and public affairs. Those who are familiar with public journalism will notice its similarities to slow journalism. In public journalism, journalists attempted to move away from the traditional journalistic norms of neutrality, distance, and objectivity to bring journalism closer to the community they served. In so doing, public journalists tried to create public "conversation," rather than supplying simple facts, and sometimes engaged in mobilizing and problem-solving tasks for the community.[40] Likewise, slow journalism seeks to provide more than daily tidbits of facts. Like public journalism, it tries to enlighten and empower its audience through collaboration. Public journalism appeared to have disappeared in the early aughts. But its offspring soon bloomed in the names of solutions journalism, constructive journalism, and engaged journalism.[41] Solutions journalism is a growing network of journalists who strive to report not just about the problems facing society but also how communities respond to them.[42] Similarly, constructive journalism avoids conflict-ridden, negative storytelling and attempts to achieve solution-focused news and provide the public with possibilities to act.[43] Engaged journalism seeks to provide the people and communities journalists cover with more agency in the process by which their stories are told.[44] These ideas are rather loosely defined, and there may be some important differences among them, but they all share the principle that journalism should be more than providing facts and information, and journalists should value a collaborative relationship with the audience they serve. And they all agree on the idea that modern journalism needs to be more mindful, have respite from time pressure, and reflect on its missions and functions in society. In other words, "slowness" can be an overarching framework of the various reform attempts of journalism, which is why I adopted it as the theoretical pillar of this chapter. In addition, the idea of slowness is broad enough to cover both the news production and the consumption aspects of journalism and is a specific counterweight to the technology craze of modern journalism.

Slow and Mindful Innovation

The speed of technological innovation in newsrooms has accelerated since the early 2000s, with high expectations coming from social media and other web 2.0 technologies. Numerous technologies and media ventures have come and gone. But failures are seldom remembered, and few lessons are learned from them. Instead, relentless innovation and experimentation are celebrated following the dubious business principle of "disruptive innovation."[45] In fact, media executives make frequent visits to Silicon Valley to learn about entrepreneurial spirit and agility in innovation.

Would such a Silicon Valley, venture capitalist mindset of innovation work for news organizations? It is difficult to say. There are successful cases of media outlets that began as a start-up backed by venture capital, such as *BuzzFeed*, but the vast majority of them have failed.[46] And as will be illustrated in the next section, the success of *BuzzFeed* is as much about its relationship with its readers as it is about technological innovation. The start-up philosophy is especially incompatible with legacy media. Silicon Valley start-ups always take huge risks, and once they hit the lottery their absolute priority becomes "growth"— they have to grow fast and achieve scale, even with losses, because building a large userbase and ecosystem is critical for their long-term survival and prosperity.[47] Such a risk-ridden venture with high failure rates and a growth-occupied model will not translate well to old-school legacy media. As media innovation and management scholar Lucy Küng explains, there are huge disparities between tech start-ups and legacy media in terms of attitudes toward risk and resources available to invest in innovation and scale.[48] Legacy media simply cannot operate with a fast-paced growth philosophy.

A high-octane model of innovation is not sustainable. In fact, journalists are experiencing unprecedented burnout in an era of perpetual short-term innovation.[49] Such was a common response expressed by journalists surveyed for the previous chapter. This is dangerous because it hurts innovation. The feelings of burnout, lethargy, and resignation prevent both the generation and the implementation of innovative ideas. The constant pressure and uncertainty may drive away dedicated newsroom personnel. Not only that, but these attempts at innovation usually come without a clear focus or careful research, and, as such, they sap resources from news organizations. More fundamentally, the fetish of speedy technological adoption relegates the larger idea of innovation to a market- and technology-driven attempt at change for the sake of economic sustainability. As the critical discourse analysis of Brian Creech and Anthony Nadler points out, the currently dominant conceptualization of innovation reveals "an inherently revenue- and market-driven logic, where it becomes synonymous with the term 'sustainability,' as in the need to develop new products, processes, and journalism that can be considered valuable enough for funders, audiences, advertisers, or sponsors to invest in."[50] Such a narrow focus precludes alternative visions of the press like that of the public journalism movement, which engages diverse publics on the ground.

That's why the idea of slowness needs to be applied not only to journalistic content and production but also to journalism's attitudes toward technology. Slow values provide newsrooms with respite from the pressures of market-driven, frenzied technological innovation and encourage revival and reflection. This is not to discourage innovations in the newsroom. On the contrary, slow values help foster innovation by making it more viable. They make us think of innovation from a long-term perspective in relation to journalism's missions and how it can be sustained.

So, what would a slow and sustainable innovation look like? Most of all, an appreciation of "mindfulness" is necessary. The idea of mindfulness originates from Buddhist philosophy and has been popularized in the West by such figures as Jon Kabat-Zinn, and it has become an important concept of the slow movement. Kabat-Zinn defines mindfulness as "the awareness that emerges through paying attention on purpose, in the present moment, and nonjudgmentally to the unfolding of experience moment by moment."[51] Mindfulness teaches newsroom personnel to slow down and live and act consciously. Some newsrooms and journalism education programs are already engaged in mindful journalism, in which they start their meetings with meditation to reflect on various events they cover and to build their resilience and moral compass.[52] Applied specifically to technology adoption and innovation, mindfulness means having a conscious purpose and goal, rather than senselessly experimenting with new and shiny things out of fear and anxiety of falling behind. Like the Middle Path in Buddhism, it means avoiding the two extremes—one with mindless indulgence in technological innovation, and the other with severe asceticism. In terms of actual practice, this means having a clear focus and research, with long-term goals connected to journalistic missions. Innovators in newsrooms should ask: What is this technology and what purpose does it serve? Does our organization *need* to adopt this technology? How does it promote journalistic functions and enhance reader experiences?

Answering those questions eventually leads to the discussion of the core missions of journalism. What is journalism, and why do we care about it?

Beyond making profits as a business, journalism serves society by informing, educating, and entertaining readers. It also monitors the powers that be
and helps build communities. Then, sustainable technological adoption and
innovation should be something that expands those missions. That should
be the clear focus of mindful journalistic innovation, which will not distract
and waste limited newsroom resources. Journalists are and should be good
at independently gathering data, evaluating and talking to sources, verifying
facts, and providing analysis and commentary on complex issues. These are
their core strengths that connect to journalism's missions and are not easily replaced. Philip Meyer, in his book *The Vanishing Newspaper: Saving Journalism in the Information Age*, argues that the ultimate way to save journalism
is not technological innovation but a return to its core functions, as mentioned above.[53] Meyer cites the well-known business case where the railroads
in the early twentieth-century United States survived the threat from trucks
on interstate highways and airlines by focusing on the one thing that they
could still do better: moving bulk cargo across long distances.[54] Likewise, the
indispensable functions and services of news organizations, which are their
core strengths, are the fundamentals of journalism serving society. As Meyer
argues, "One of the rules of thumb for coping with substitute technology is
to narrow your focus to the area that is the least vulnerable to substitution.
. . . What service supplied by newspapers is the least vulnerable? I still
believe . . . that a newspaper's most important product, the product least vulnerable to substitution, is community influence. It gains this influence by
being the trusted source for locally produced news, analysis and investigative reporting about public affairs. This influence makes it more attractive
to advertisers."[55]

Due to the nature of the journalism business serving a democratic society, innovation in journalism relates to even larger concerns. Media in general, and journalism in particular, do not just reflect but also promote societal
changes. As Axel Bruns argues, media organizations are "intermediate and
do mediate between different parts of society, and as society changes, so do
the media which are situated in between its constituent elements. In a very
direct sense, therefore, when we examine media innovations, we are really
investigating one of the processes of societal innovation."[56] This is a holis-
tic, ecological view of the media-social system, very much in line with a key
doctrine of Buddhist philosophy—"mutual dependencies," or "dependent
co-arising," which is the belief that everything exists because other things
exist. In this view, mindful journalism and innovation look at "the mass communication system as an essential component of an interdependent,

interconnected, and interactive whole operating at several hierarchical levels—the community, the nation-state, the world, the universe, and variations within this range."[57] Therefore, journalistic innovation is more than simple changes in technologies or practices. It is connected to larger social systems and societal evolutions.

The quest for journalistic innovation produces philosophical questions: What do we want our society to be? What kind of a news system do we need for democracy? Who does journalism serve? In an age where frenzied speed dictates much of their lives, journalists and newsroom innovators should pause and consider what it means to produce good journalism and what the missions and identities of journalism in society should be.

Innovation with and Beyond Technology

In 1982, critics derided a new journalistic venture as dumb because of its plain writing style and bold use of color, and they predicted that it would fail. What were they talking about? *USA Today*. This newspaper that critics said was dumbing down Americans would grow into the country's darling, boasting one of the largest circulations in the industry. And it inspired a generation of journalists and many news organizations in its wake. The success of *USA Today* is a well-known story. What was the main reason it became so successful? It wasn't technology. It was the paper's unique design and writing style, which were friendly and accessible to the readers it served. It understood well what the readers wanted. Media scholars George Sylvie and Patricia Witherspoon, who did an ethnographic study of the *USA Today* newsroom, explain that the paper was successful because it embraced risk-taking and celebrated difference while remaining quality-conscious.[58] They argue that from the start, the vision of founder Al Neuharth to make a friendly newspaper different from the elitist publications was taken up by the employees and transformed into something bigger. In so doing, the culture of bottom-up collaboration prevailed during the innovation process. Instead of infusing the newsroom with MBA-led, top-down changes, the managers of *USA Today* encouraged self-autonomy and normative changes among journalists, according to Sylvie and Witherspoon. In other words, *USA Today*'s innovation mainly came from a different mindset toward its readership, and it was enabled by the appropriate culture and people within the organization.

A similar thing happened in the late 2000s when *BuzzFeed* began. The outlet was once derided as a site full of cheap, lighthearted, nonserious entertainment content—a site where you would go to see some cute kittens or silly jokes. Yes, it became famous with advertiser-supported listicles and quizzes. Today, however, *BuzzFeed* has become a top news site in the United States and one of the world's largest producers of digital content, with employees and offices worldwide.[59] It now produces award-winning, serious investigative and in-depth news reports around the world. It has had journalists on the ground in Kyiv to break stories on the Ukrainian crisis. It proved that operatives with apparent ties to Vladimir Putin have engaged in a targeted killing campaign against his perceived enemies on British and American soil.[60] Its investigative reporting on how corporate executives convicted of crimes escape punishment using a sketchy legal system had an impact on public policy changes.[61] It broke a mindboggling story on how torture and sexual abuse were rampant in an orphanage in Vermont run by nuns.[62] In fact, *BuzzFeed* has become one of the best investigative, in-depth reporting news agencies that brings original and previously less-explored issues to the fore. That's why it has received numerous honors, ranging from a National Magazine Award in the category of Public Interest to National Press Foundation awards.

The success of *BuzzFeed* comes from many directions. The outlet is certainly technology-driven, with a culture and mindset in line with those in Silicon Valley. *BuzzFeed* uses sophisticated technology and data science techniques to analyze user data and predict and produce viral content. On *BuzzFeed*, "user data are captured, analyzed, and manipulated in a perpetual loop of analysis, interpretation, experimentation, feedback, and refinement."[63] Its investigative reporting also often uses powerful data analytics to identify suspicious patterns in events.[64]

But the technology alone does not explain its enormous success. *Buzz-Feed* is "a tech-media hybrid, and *BuzzFeed*'s content is both an art and a science."[65] Beyond the technology, it breaks the mold and brings transformation in terms of coverage, newsroom personnel, and operation. *BuzzFeed* differentiated itself by first devoting a lot of space to social issues, such as the LGBTQ experience, civil rights, gender equality, and drug legislation, which captured the minds of young readers. Rather than neglecting such areas or lumping them into other, larger assignments—as is done by mainstream news organizations—it designated them as separate news beats that merited having their own assigned reporters.[66] While it employs a predominantly young staff, the organization has also brought in high-profile senior figures, blending youth and experience.[67] In terms of reporting, it was found that *BuzzFeed* quotes ordinary citizens more often than does the mainstream media, and this is facilitated by new communication technologies, as users post their opinions and even their own breaking news on social media sites.[68] And most *BuzzFeed* reports are written in a fun, engaging, and accessible style, which has brought in new readers. In sum, *BuzzFeed*'s successful innovation comes from not just the utilization of technology but also innovation in organization and respect for user experience.

Yet another successful example of digital newsroom innovation is the *Guardian*. The British legacy newspaper successfully transitioned from a quality domestic newspaper to a digital powerhouse and global leader in journalism. As of 2019, it boasts about 160 million unique visitors to its various websites worldwide.[69] It has produced many impactful data and digital journalism pieces, and its in-depth coverage of such events as the Edward Snowden–National Security Agency scandal and the COVID-19 pandemic has received many accolades. How was the *Guardian* able to reinvent itself as a top news organization in the digital age? Scholars point to several factors, including strategic control, careful research, and a self-reflexive culture.[70] Lucy Küng, in particular, argues that a combination of different yet interconnected factors, including culture, leadership, technology, and strategies, have produced a success: acknowledging the crowded British domestic market and omnipresence of the BBC, the *Guardian* strategically sought growth in international markets, aiming for a clearly defined audience—a global target market for English-speaking, youngish, liberal, intelligent people. In doing so, it strongly held on to its mission, seeing itself as a serious journalistic endeavor, one that would stand up to authority when necessary, which translated to a serious commitment to investigative and in-depth reporting. The visionary leadership of Alan Rusbridger and Emily Bell facilitated these efforts. Most of all, Küng explains, the newspaper's governance system—the Scott Trust Limited—set the tone for the leadership approach and corporate culture conducive to innovation as well as serious journalism. The Scott Trust began as a charitable foundation and sought to ensure the paper's editorial independence in perpetuity while maintaining its financial health. It is the paper's guiding light that ensures its journalistic freedom and liberal values. The Trust promoted a newsroom culture that is characterized by minimal hierarchy, an open-management style, and a tradition of board consultation where a staff ballot is part of the decision-making process. As such, the Trust has been the bedrock of the *Guardian*'s culture and may have prescribed the paper's successful innovation paths.[71]

It would be a mistake to think that innovation in journalism is synonymous with the advancement of technology—how technology improves the production and dissemination of news. All the cases above attest to the fact

Chart 4 Multiple dimensions of innovation

that successful journalistic innovation is more than technology adoption and utilization. A slew of research from management, organizational science, and media studies also suggests that journalistic innovation is innovation in practices, structures, and operations as much as in technologies.[72] And often it is more the interactions between technology, individuals, and structures, than technology per se, that produce organizational changes. Social studies of technological change, such as the adaptive structuration theory described in the introduction, indicate that the outcomes of technology incorporation to work settings are largely determined by local dynamics consisting of human agency and social structures.[73] That was certainly the case for the *Guardian*, *USA Today*, and *BuzzFeed*.

Technology is only one part of journalistic innovation, and other factors and their interdependencies should be considered for successful organizational change and innovation. As chart 4 illustrates, innovation can happen among many different facets, sometimes at the same time, blending, for example, new technology tools with new practices of audience engagement.[74] Likewise, Lucy Küng, who in another work studied five successful digital innovators in journalism—the *New York Times*, *Quartz*, *Vice*, the *Guardian*, and *BuzzFeed*—concludes that the common patterns found in those organizations were strong purpose and leadership; focused strategies; a blending of journalistic, technological, and business competencies; and a culture conducive to digital innovation, and that these factors were combined and operated in a virtuous circle.[75]

A similar perspective was found among many rank-and-file journalists, not management, about what makes for effective newsroom innovation. In the survey introduced in chapter 2, reporters were also asked to what extent they thought various types of innovations in journalism are important. In their view, technology was among the least important dimensions of innovation. What the reporters found the most important in innovation was people and culture, including leadership. Many reporters were frustrated that their newsroom culture is too rigid to be receptive to new ideas, and that any new ideas under consideration tend to be forced on them from the top down. Therefore, it is important to understand multifaceted dimensions of newsroom innovation, beyond technology.

Culture, Norms, and People in Newsroom Innovation

It is beyond the scope of this book to discuss all these different dimensions of innovation in detail—after all, this is not a work about management science. But I'd like to provide some observations on the roles of people—both news workers and audience—and newsroom norms and culture in innovation, because these are the dimensions deemed important by the reporters in the survey, and they are also directly relevant to the core strengths of journalism.

First, newsroom norms and culture are critical in successful journalistic innovation. Many previous studies suggest that professional newsroom culture is often at odds with innovation in the industry.[76] Peter Gade, for example, found that innovation, usually initiated by management, frequently presented threats to the self-autonomous culture of journalists and their professional journalistic norms, which resulted in resistance to change, creating a fundamental dichotomy between journalistic and business-technology ideals.[77] Culture, in those studies, is a strong hindrance to innovation. But this also means that when utilized properly, culture can become the most important catalyst of innovation in newsroom. There is a great deal of scholarship in management and organizational science about creating a culture amenable to innovation. For example, a classic text in organizational change suggests that effective implementation of change includes a collaborative culture in an organization, which includes coalition-building; articulation of a shared vision; ensuring communication education and training; enabling participation and innovation; providing symbols, signals, and rewards; and ensuring standards, measures, and feedback mechanisms.[78] Similar characteristics can be found in digitally innovative organizations: less hierarchical and more distributed in leadership structure; more collaborative and cross-functional; and encouraging of experimentation and learning, to name a few.[79] Sylvie and Witherspoon, who did an in-depth study of *USA Today*, found that those elements were embodied in the newspaper's culture during its successful launch.[80] As they explained, the managers of *USA Today* recognized existing newsroom culture and routines, cherished them, took advantage of them, and eventually used them in creating new routines. What they improved involved not only production-oriented tasks but also a newspaper's spirit, its identity, the conventional ways in which it views itself, its rituals of newsgathering, and its persona.[81] Likewise, the *Guardian*'s less hierarchical, open culture was conducive to digital innovation, and thus its transition from print to digital went much more smoothly than those of many of its legacy competitors.[82] Overall, to achieve a meaningful and sustainable journalistic innovation, a newsroom climate of trust is needed to allow people to learn, experiment, and dare to disagree.[83] It is important to have insights on how professionals in the newsroom actually learn and innovate, to what extent a culture of learning exists, and how much it allows them to learn and innovate in the first place.[84] This way, innovative ideas that promote journalistic missions will be facilitated.

Even with an open, learning, and collaborative newsroom culture, however, successful innovation requires ongoing negotiations of professional journalistic norms. It has been found that changes that journalists see as beneficial to their understanding of the field are viewed favorably, while journalists are resistant to changes they believe challenge journalistic autonomy and judgment and hurt the quality of the news product.[85] As such, traditional norms, such as autonomy, are negotiated against the value of innovation, and they can often hinder or facilitate innovation. For example, a recent study of 360° video adoption in newsrooms found that despite its utility and relative ease of production, journalists find that it conflicts with such journalistic norms as accuracy, autonomy, and control; they find that in a 360° video, the viewer's freedom to choose the field of view can lead to a less accurate picture of the story and a loss of the journalist's control of the content, which has hindered the technology's adoption.[86] Similar results can be found elsewhere such that the professional culture of traditional journalism has a strong inertia in the online newsrooms and has prevented journalists from developing most of the ideals of interactivity, as such an innovation did not fit in the standardized news production routines.[87] What this means is that if a viable technological innovation is to take place, it has to either (1) conform to and facilitate existing norms, routines, and cultural practices of the newsroom, or (2) transform the mindset of those in the newsroom, "many times unlearning the trade and its institutional truths."[88] It can be argued that the cases of *USA Today* and the *Guardian* represent those where the innovation conformed to and enhanced existing norms within the newsroom. As Sylvie and Witherspoon pointed out, a collaborative learning culture already existed at *USA Today*, and managers only had to facilitate it with a strong vision and principles.[89] And the innovation *USA Today* pursued related to journalism's core mission of informing and engaging the audience. As noted above, its design, writing style, and curation of topics were the products of the staff's response to the desires of its readers, which helped encourage reader engagement. For the *Guardian*, its liberal values, embedded in the Scott Trust and its news operation, have only been enhanced following successful digitization. The paper's governance system and normative structures meant that it must move forward while respecting and keeping continuity with its past, but such existing norms were compatible with the emerging global digital ecosystem: an open, participatory newsroom with liberal progressive values fits nicely with the culture of digital natives and digital disrupters.[90] The case of *BuzzFeed*, on the contrary, is closer to the transformation of culture, which is less common. The company's start-up roots and young workforce, who often do not have a background in journalism, may have allowed transformative norms within the newsroom, quite different from traditional outlets. From the use of listicles to news quizzes and content backed by machine learning, *BuzzFeed* pushed the idea of what journalism is and what it can be. Although it has become more like a traditional news outlet these days, playing by the rules of the journalistic field, it surely has pushed the boundaries of the industry. Another notable case in this "transformation" category is the American digital business news site *Quartz* and its parent group, Atlantic Media. The company is said to have achieved successful digital transformation by "pretending it was a Silicon Valley start-up that needed to kill itself to survive."[91]

Because changes in news organizations are implemented, ultimately, through their organizational members, the newsroom culture and development of people have to be strongly fused to achieve successful innovation. News workers, such as reporters, editors, photographers, and programmers, play a significant role in spreading, explaining, and interpreting new technologies and in forging the understanding of future trends.[92] Management scholarship thus emphasizes that organizational change is all about people: innovative organizations value employees' experience and knowledge, and empower them to seek change themselves. In such an environment, employees then develop "absorptive capacity," an ability to recognize the value of new ideas and assimilate them for successful organizational change and innovation.[93] That was the case with *USA Today*, where management empowered its employees, and change was personified in the very people who worked there.[94] But there are plenty of cases of failure due to overlooking the people in the newsroom. For example, at the *St. Louis Post-Dispatch*, a reform movement in the late 1990s to change its beat system to a team-based model failed, as journalists did not feel empowered in the new setup.[95] Similarly, as shown in Joyce Nip's study of the last days of public journalism at the *Savannah Morning News*, the values of public journalism were imposed on individual journalists, rather than forming part of the broad organization of newswork, which made it difficult for rank-and-file team members to buy into the philosophy.[96] The success of innovation and change, after all, will require the collaboration and commitment of the people who compose organizations.

Moving on to the audience side, innovation in audience engagement is perhaps the most valuable and fundamental aspect of innovation today. As discussed above, some of the most powerful reform movements in journalism—public journalism, solutions journalism, engaged journalism—have been attempts to reconfigure journalism's relationship to its audience. They are about reimagining an audience as members of the public, competent citizens, and collaborators. For too long, news organizations have treated the audience as mere "customers" to whom they deliver their predetermined news products. In the heyday of newspaper business, Sylvie and Witherspoon made this critical observation:

> Newspapers view their readers as customers. The view is built on the assumption that reading is all a customer can do with a newspaper, that reading is the only activity involved in the use of a

newspaper. Of course, this is not true. The public interacts with the newspaper in myriad ways. Yet reading, or more accurately, subscribing, is the primary action the industry seeks when it attempts to measure success. In this approach, then, the industry views the physical newspaper as its product, when, in fact, newspapers produce more than a rolled-up compilation of graphic devices that gets tossed on a porch or a lawn. Why cannot readers be considered news connoisseurs instead? Why does the newspaper industry need to be concerned with people who read or who read on a regular basis? In short, the newspaper should be viewed as an experience, not necessarily just a product.[97]

Things are not too different in the digital age. News organizations are still lost about the idea of the audience as real people and tend to regard them as numbers showing up in data analytics. Growing and managing as many people as possible and generating content that appeals to audiences has become a core practice of digital journalism today. But how many of those billions of likes and shares appearing in the analytics actually convert to loyal readers? Does the audience really want the algorithmically produced information pandering to their low tastes? How are those analytics furthering the journalistic mission of providing audiences with the information needed to self-govern in a democracy?

Recent innovations in audience engagement tell a lot about the importance of building a collaborative and appreciative relationship with the audience. The German weekly *Die Zeit* capitalizes its smart userbase by offering conferences, classes, and even career services and art products.[98] The same goes for the *New Yorker*, which holds an annual festival of ideas and discussions on literature, politics, and popular culture. Their not-so-cheap tickets for the festival events usually sell out quickly and are an important source of revenue.[99] Most of all, it is an important venue for audience appreciation and development, where new readers are acquired and existing readers celebrate their camaraderie. These endeavors help media outlets like the *New Yorker* and *Die Zeit* become more trusted sources of news and encourage people to pay premium subscription prices. Most stories reported in the *New Yorker* are features written from the first-person perspective, often with the writers' very subjective interpretation and analysis. How do the readers know that these first-person, personally driven stories are actually true? They don't. They trust the stories because they believe in the journalists and their publication. Such trust is enhanced by the outlet's appreciation of its readers. All in all, these endeavors help the audience view news organizations as a positive "experience," not just a product.

Beyond commercial news outlets, some public media are engaged in noble attempts to invigorate their relationship with audiences. Alaska Public Media's Community in Unity project reaches out to a broad spectrum of listeners, especially seeking minority voices—including prisoners—in the community, and has organized in-person conversations on local issues. The project then sought persistent input from the audience by, for example, sending thank-you notes to the participants and returning to the prisons to conduct follow-up interviews with the inmates, which built trust with them and has prompted correspondence with multiple people who are still incarcerated or have recently been released.[100] Capital Public Radio in Sacramento, California, a city plagued with a housing crisis, partnered with community organizations and hosted "story circles" to bring together renters, homeowners, developers, and homeless people who would share their personal stories. Their in-person gathering featured food, candles, and a centerpiece placed in the middle of the circle, such as a bouquet of flowers, to give participants a shared object of contemplation.[101] In yet another example of sincere audience engagement, reporters and editors participated in the Knight Foundation's On the Table initiative, a program that connected neighbors over mealtime conversations on pressing community issues, where local journalists worked as moderators to facilitate difficult discussions and then used the gatherings as a way to connect with the audience.[102]

To varying degrees, those examples are cases of a more meaningful engagement that regards the audience as more than customers. Such approaches to audience engagement are dubbed "relational," as opposed to "transactional."[103] Relational engagement is an audience engagement on the ground, building networks and holding community discussion, which is a more collaborative and sustainable relationship with the audience. These efforts may or may not come with the help of technology. If any technology helps promote relational audience engagement, it should be utilized, as shown in the exemplary case of Hearken, a digital platform that helps news organizations gather audience questions and inputs to find out what the public would like reporters to cover. But the cases introduced above provide interesting insight into the future of audience engagement and digital technologies. That is, these news organizations were engaged in old-fashioned, face-to-face gatherings among journalists and audiences through conferences, workshops, and community discussion, especially before the COVID-19 pandemic.[104] Typically, it has been the case that the engagement buzz is associated with mass digital tactics, where newsrooms use analytics to reach the largest possible audience and interact with them via social media platforms. But even digital native newsrooms are increasingly focusing on offline relationship-building, designed to support collaborative action, as shown in a recent ethnography of engaged newsrooms.[105] This is because online platforms today can produce myriad problems, such as harassment, hate speech, and privacy invasion, plus open, mass online engagement has often resulted in empty reach. Therefore, these newsrooms are coming full circle, "remembering the importance of forging deeper, narrower, and stronger relationships with their audiences, emphasizing physical encounter and investment in niche audiences over scale."[106] No matter how rich and complete data analytics are, actually taking time to talk to people may produce unexpected insights and deeper understanding of the audience.

Successful technological innovation and audience engagement in journalism require careful planning and long-term commitment, understanding the people and culture on the ground. Practitioners of journalism need to think about the industry's pace and direction. Going slow will not make them lag behind. Actually, a slower, more mindful pace may make news organizations more competitive. That is, in the media environment characterized by information overload and quick-fix products to attract user attention, going slow and creating lasting values will be more beneficial to news organizations in the long run. News agencies can convert random visitors to loyal subscribers by providing journalistic products that readers can trust and appreciate. And such efforts will come not just from technological innovation but also from innovations in organization, people, culture, and audience engagement.

This chapter probed what sustainable and mindful innovation means in journalism and how news organizations may achieve it. As a background philosophy, the idea of "slow" was applied to news production as well as to innovation. The increasingly frenetic pace of modern life and capitalism has subjected every facet of society, including newsrooms and the idea of technological innovation, to cutthroat competition and a relentless pursuit of speed. Today, the discourse of speed has become a natural way of understanding technologies in journalism.[107] But as this happens, we see the negative consequences of fast living and unfettered capitalism. In journalism, the quality of news products and, accordingly, people's trust in news media have plummeted, and journalists are experiencing burnout, stress, and heightened pressure to be more productive and efficient. More importantly, neither the purpose nor the mission of journalism is appreciated in the fast-paced changes toward commercial ends.

If news organizations want to be truly competitive, they should step back, focus on their core strengths, and build products that regain trust from the audience they serve. That's a good, clean, and more sustainable journalism, although one that moves slowly.

Conclusion

In Search of Journalism's Identities

> We have histories of everything about journalism except journalism itself.
>
> —James Carey

In the middle of the COVID-19 pandemic in 2020, the *Washington Post* published a stunning interactive visualization in which moving dots represented people in a city.[1] The dots were color-coded, so that gray represented uninfected ones, red represented infected ones, and pink represented those who had acquired immunity. The simulator showed that whenever a red dot touched a gray dot, the gray turned red, which made it abundantly clear that without social distancing and other intervention measures, the whole field quickly became full of red dots. It was informative and interesting, and it transmitted important messages about public health. Mesmerized, I played it several times. This visualization is indeed a prime example of effective data journalism and visualization, which is probably the most celebrated journalistic genre in recent years. Then again, I cannot help feeling that the visualization is rather too simple: the model looks too neat to explain the spread of this monstrous and mysterious virus. But I couldn't tell what exactly was missing from the story. My question was answered when Siddhartha Mukherjee, a renowned physician and medical journalist, wrote a powerful analysis for the *New Yorker*. There he suggested that most reports, given the paucity of data, have been forced to model the spread of the new coronavirus as if it were a binary phenomenon: individuals are either exposed or unexposed, infected or uninfected, symptomatic patients or asymptomatic carriers. In a subtle critique of the *Washington Post* visualization model, Mukherjee wondered, "The doctor and medical researcher in me—as a graduate student, I was trained in viral immunology—wanted to know what was going on *within* the dots. How much virus was in *that* red dot? How fast was it replicating in *this* dot? How was the exposure—the 'touch time'—related to the chance of transmission? How long did a red dot remain red—that is, how did an individual's infectiousness change over time? And what was the severity of the disease in each case?"[2] In other words, the beautiful visualization cannot explain the complexity of the virus and is maybe even misleading. No wonder the *Post*'s visualization is powerful. And this kind of story has its own efficacy and importance. The visualization will reach many people and have a powerful impact; few people would read the 4,500-word essay by Mukherjee in the *New Yorker*, which many consider elitist. Yet I learned so much more about the virus from Mukherjee's story. His work is that of an expert and an artist, blending detailed scientific expertise and journalistic elegance, produced using only written words. The *Post*'s story is probably more appealing and interesting, but which helps us better understand the complicated nature of this virus?

This is where contemporary journalism driven by technology suffers the most. Again, it is not to discount the efficacy of data journalism and visualization itself—it is a powerful tool of contemporary journalists to help them provide unique and approachable insights to readers. However, technology-driven mindsets may crowd out important functions of journalism. In pursuit of nimble digital adaptation and content that may appeal to the most people, it is increasingly hard to find in-depth stories written by expert journalists who can provide context, meaning, and clarity to complex events, and therefore better serve the interest of the public. The scientific community has long warned against outbreaks of global epidemics, be it a novel coronavirus or an avian flu. Why didn't the news media put such important warnings at the forefront and play a watchdog role, pointing out the government's unpreparedness? Why were they not able to report that there would be a shortage of masks and ventilators because the government had reduced subsidies and funding, and companies relocated their production overseas for cheap labor? If there were more seasoned public health and policy experts in newsrooms, and executives and management had been less bothered by short-term profit goals and recognized the importance of journalism in public life, we might have better prepared for the COVID-19 pandemic. If journalism operated more slowly, considering its public missions rather than being caught by a frenzied technology feast, we might have saved more lives. This may be wild conjecture but it is still worth pondering.

I haven't discussed in-depth data journalism and visualization—currently one of the greatest infatuations in journalism—because they are more a question of renewed practices rather than material technologies. But the thesis of this book applies to data journalism and related technologies and practices as well: with all their great potential and benefit, the industry is going too fast, mostly focusing on greater tool development and utilization rather than contemplating what they mean for journalism and journalists, and how they can improve civic and democratic missions of journalism.

In data journalism, big data and sophisticated data-processing algorithms enable previously unimaginable reporting with engaging visuals, which can greatly aid readers' understanding of events. But an emphasis on attractive visuals and data-processing tools may come at the expense of a critical understanding of data and what data journalism should be. After years of research and practice, trial and error, we now know that data and data processing is not neutral, and they will reproduce or even exacerbate biases and problems present in modern society.[3] In the process of data collection, storage, analysis, and presentation, existing power and social relations are at work such that who collects and processes data, and who analyzes data in what way, influences the construction and interpretation of data.[4] In other words, data does not exist in a vacuum but is socially constructed, much like other technologies discussed throughout this book. If so, perhaps what is more important for data journalism is to report *on* data and algorithms rather than *with* data and algorithms. Data journalists should be more attuned to probing what is and what is not included in data and how data and algorithms reproduce or exacerbate social biases and inequalities. Currently, work exploring social justice and serving democracy is sparse.[5] But that's probably where data journalism can shine the brightest and help reclaim journalism's cultural authority in the public sphere.

The same goes for social media—another dominant obsession of journalism in our time—which enables a set of new practices for journalists. Social media has been considered a boon for journalism due to its potential to increase transparency and openness and its powerful ability to circulate news quickly. Not only that, but social media also allows journalists to reach and engage with both wider and niche audiences. Its ability to quickly spread citizen-generated content against authoritarian regimes is even credited with the rise of democratization movements around the world, such as the Arab Spring.[6] Traditional journalists' use of social media during the democratization movements was also revolutionary, as they were shown to use much more nonelite and alternative sources in their reporting.[7] Due to its many presumed benefits, using social media has become imperative for many news organizations. As Seth Lewis and Logan Molyneux documented in their observation of newsrooms, supervisors urge journalists to use social media and then monitor their accounts: "If you are not on Twitter, get an account already—and make sure you have at least a few hundred followers by the end of the year. We'll be tracking your activity."[8]

But things change so fast in the technology world. Once-cool social media in recent years has become a fertile breeding ground of misinformation, conspiracy theories, misogyny, and creepy privacy invasion. The interactivity and engagement between journalists and audiences on social media have quickly turned into harassment and trolling of journalists.[9] The Arab Spring brought about by the Twitter revolution turned into the Arab Winter, or a resurgence of authoritarian power and control that squelched the democratization movement.[10]

The rise and fall of social media—and the binary arguments that social media either brings revolution or not; enhances openness or not; spreads misinformation or not; transforms journalistic work or not—attest to the dominant industry discourse to consider technology as a savior of journalism. As such, these are heavily technology-deterministic viewpoints that do not consider the importance of the social conditions in which social media is embedded. For example, it was not the social media per se that brought the democratic revolution and the counterrevolution. The Arab Spring had deep underlying causes and was prefigured over many years, and the emergence of social media only facilitated the actual organization of protests.[11] It was never the case that the technology alone achieved the revolution, although it allowed new methods of organization and protest unavailable using traditional media. The same is true for the argument that social media causes the wide spread of fake news, a point of view that barely considers the underlying social, cultural, and political conditions under which fake news emerges in the first place.

In prioritizing social media tools and activities, journalists and journalism scholars are less likely to reflect on the industry's inner workings and its mission to address societal concerns. As Lewis and Molyneux argue, "time spent analyzing tweets could be coming at the expense of analyzing the logics of algorithms, the political economy of technology giants, and other organizational and institutional arrangements that are reshaping the contexts for news subsidy."[12]

This book began with the critique of the *New York Times*'s "Snow Fall" in 2012, a marvelous digital story that barely considered optimal user experience. Since then, a relatively long time, from the perspective of the fast-evolving techno-journalism world, has passed. Numerous media-technology start-ups have come and gone. *Upworthy*, once a darling on Facebook, is now hard to find; the hyped citizen social news platform *Fresco News* is gone; and when I was about to start this book, the Civil blockchain launched with fanfare, but it folded midway through my writing. Material technologies have been evolving so fast that readers today enjoy all different types of storytelling and news products, ranging from news games to 3D animations and tactile stimulations. The pursuit of technological adoption and innovation only continues to grow. But this relentless chase of technology begs an important question: Is technology a vital element of what is meant by journalism? What constitutes good journalism? Ultimately, this leads to questions about the core identities of journalism. I have provided some answers to these questions here and there in the preceding chapters, but in this concluding section I will weave together the arguments presented so far, hoping to better understand what journalism means for society.

Few other industries have been more affected by the technological revolution than journalism. It is a common belief that the telegraph produced a new form of writing; photographs and visual media redefined the value of news; the internet brought down the newspaper business; artificial intelligence is replacing human reporters; the utilization of big data and sophisticated analytic science is producing a new kind of journalism; drones are providing footage previously impossible to obtain; and so forth. Indeed, what we call news today is quite different from the news of a century ago. Technology transformed what is meant by journalists, too, such that ordinary citizens engaging in newswork with new media tools challenge professional journalists.

Then again, nothing has changed in journalism. Reporters—whether professional or citizen—still gather information following certain standards and provide it to the audience. They talk to and interact with sources, whether people or big data; try to write a compelling narrative, whether with written words or multimedia; and distribute news, whether via carrier pigeon or cable. The fundamentals of journalism have remained pretty stable for much of the field's history.

How is that possible? How can technology have changed everything in journalism and also not have changed anything at all? The answer stems from the instrumental view of technology. Because the journalism industry has been dominated by the discourse of how technology transforms journalism and how it can utilize technology for efficient innovation and commercial gain, these seemingly contradictory positions came to regard "change and continuity as two sides of the same transformational coin."[13] That is, journalists have believed that journalistic transformation through technology is necessary so that they can keep doing what they have been doing.

It is in this discourse of continuity and change by technology that those in the industry talk when they refer to journalistic innovation. But this view connotes a narrow view of innovation because, in such a discourse, innovation is signified as visions of journalism that adhere to the forces of technology influenced by market dynamics.[14] Here, the function of technology is equated to speeding up the news process to generate revenue and maintain a viable business. As Henrik Örnebring argues, "the discourse of speed, understood as at heart a capitalist logic of competition and use of technology to increase productivity, has become a wholly naturalized element of journalism and forms a template for how journalists understand new technologies."[15]

As the discourse analysis of journalism and technology in chapter 2 demonstrated, the quest to make journalism stay afloat under tough economic conditions and to fend off outsiders threatening the legitimacy of the journalistic field resulted in an overemphasis on the mythical power of technology. But this narrow and particularistic view of journalistic innovation tied to technology and market logic presents serious threats to journalism and may hurt its future. As shown in the previous chapter, the success of such outlets as *USA Today*, the *Guardian*, and *BuzzFeed* comes mostly from cultural transformation in newsrooms and a revamped relationship with the audience, rather than from shiny technologies. But a focus on technological adoption and use may sap already limited newsroom resources and hurt the future operation of newsrooms. From the videotex experiment of the 1970s to Google Glass and conversational chatbots in recent years, the list of unsuccessful newsroom technologies is rapidly growing. How much have newsrooms learned from those failures?

Technology's impact may be indirect, unexpected, and sometimes undesirable. And as chapter 1 illustrated, even transformative technologies in journalism have gradually evolved, and their impact has been moderated by the web of organizational, cultural, and societal factors. Therefore, a slow and mindful approach to technological innovation, which entails careful research and puts the core values and strengths of journalism into consideration, is needed. Granted, the strong pressures of such tech giants as Google and Facebook, which are encroaching on the journalistic field, compel news organizations to commit to further technological innovation in search of speed and efficiency. At the end of the day, however, news organizations are not tech companies. They operate with different principles and logic. And in terms of technological innovation, they are not likely to win against tech giants, who will always have superior technologies and resources. Then, journalism's more viable way to survive vis-à-vis tech companies is to resort to innovations that enhance its core strengths, which usually come from innovations in culture, organization, people, and audience relationships.

What are journalism's core strengths, then? What are journalism's most enduring values? Do such things even exist? Comprehending the core identities of journalism is a daunting, if not impossible, task because journalism is not a monolithic, universal concept. There are so many adjectives that come before the word journalism. In terms of subjects, we see a vast array of topics, such as science, sports, business, entertainment, and environmental journalism, to name a few. In terms of media type, we see adjectives like print, broadcast, web, online, radio, et cetera. The debate on who can become a journalist produced such adjectives as professional, citizen, and pro-am (pro-amateur). Not only that, but the reform movements in journalism have brought such ideas as public, civic, solutions, engaged, and constructive journalism. And the list goes on: investigative, watchdog, mainstream, trustee, developmental, peace, literary, opinion, cultural, community . . .

The existence of so many types of journalism alludes to the idea that many have tried to change, improve, or transform journalism's operation, probably because it has not been working well. The fact that many realized this shows that people have certain standards and expectations about what journalism should do for society. Those standards and expectations may constitute what is close to the core identities of journalism. But they also vary and are not easily agreed upon. David Weaver and colleagues, who have conducted extensive surveys of journalistic values, roles, and identities over decades, argue that there is too much disagreement on journalistic norms and values to claim an emergence of overarching occupational standards in journalism, although they do see some common patterns among Western liberal democracies.[16]

The common roles and standards of journalism found in Western liberal democracies are related to a model of journalism providing information in an objective and rational manner, but such a model can be criticized as privileging the Anglo-Saxon capitalist model of informational journalism.[17] The form of journalism as we know it today, as Michael Schudson points out, is a byproduct of the Enlightenment and Western modernity that valued objective methods and rational procedures.[18] This model of journalism, although under serious challenge, still remains as a prevalent form. Now, what's added to this dominant idea of journalism is the discourse of further rationalization, efficiency, and speeding up through technology. As this happens, we forget why journalism exists and why it matters for society. Technology- and market-focused innovations relegate journalism's normative and democratic concerns to the margins. Therefore, recognizing the normative and democratic concerns would help reconstitute journalism's core identities.

Although the normative link between journalism and democracy is not inseparable, and perhaps too much emphasis on that link is not desirable, it is true that journalism has always been associated with the public and democratic life.[19] Democracy and journalism, for most of history, have evolved together normatively and, to an extent, empirically.[20] As such, invigorating the public sphere with useful information and encouraging citizen engagement can certainly be one of journalism's core missions. It is in this context that the veteran journalism practitioner-academics Bill Kovach and Tom Rosenstiel, in their classic book *The Elements of Journalism*, argued that the primary purpose of journalism is to provide citizens with the information they need to be free and self-governing.[21] Or, in Barbie Zelizer's words, journalism's raison d'être is to independently gather information for the public good and betterment of community.[22]

In the midst of the heightened pressure of commercialization, where journalistic advancement is framed according to quickly evolving technological innovation, journalism's democratic concerns are relegated to the margins. Much of the crisis in today's journalism stems from the industry itself, such that it deserted its civic missions and resorted to sensational, quick, money-grabbing reportage, which resulted in the public's disenchantment with and distrust of news media. As the two seasoned Danish journalists who studied more than fifty newsrooms in nine countries for a year concluded, the current crisis of journalism is deeper than technological. As they observed, "The crisis of journalism and legacy news media is structural, and not just a matter of technological challenges or broken business models. When citizens of Western societies, to a deeply disturbing extent, turn their backs on original news journalism, spend less time on news on radio and television, buy fewer newspapers, and express a growing distrust of media institutions, we need to submit the core content of the news media—journalism itself—to a critical review."[23] Mainstream journalism is in crisis, primarily because its media conglomerates' strong profit-driven logic caused too much commercialization and entertainmentization of news, which ultimately led to the erosion of the public trust in the profession; it is in crisis because of increasingly difficult working conditions and burdens on individual journalists, who find it difficult to fulfill their civic roles in society. But by obsessively resorting to technological innovation, journalism avoids looking at the profession's structural problems and its self-inflicted wounds. It downplays journalism's value in advancing civic and democratic concerns by which it can regain the public's trust. By celebrating technology, the industry "frames the contemporary crisis of journalism as a problem to be solved by the entrepreneurial ingenuity of firms, managers, and individual journalists, rather than broader public engagement."[24]

Democracy, which journalism purports to serve, is a slow and painful process. Unlike autocracy, where dictators can efficiently control the crowd and quickly execute policies, democracy requires arduous reasoning and deliberative processes within institutions. Court processes and elections take time, too, and representatives and policies are constantly scrutinized and often recalled. If journalism is democracy's true significant other, then it will have to pace itself to be in sync with its partner's slow steps. Journalism's hurried and harried strides only cause sensationalism, recklessness, and fatigue, and may hurt its partner.

Technologies—especially digital ones—have changed how things operate in many spheres of society. But no matter how the modalities have changed, teachers still teach and students still learn so that young people can realize their human potential and become fruitful members of society. Conventional or digital politics is still about conciliating diverse interests and values in the pursuit of better governance. Why would journalism be any different in the digital age? Again, as Kovach and Rosenstiel argue, every generation creates its own journalism, largely in reaction to technological advances that allow production and/or distribution of content more effectively, but the purpose and the underlying elements of journalism have proven remarkably constant.[25] The history of journalism and technology also tells us the importance of human agency and institutions in shaping technology. It shows that "reporters and editors are resilient and creative, even if business models and tech tools continue to change their occupation and even if their newsrooms transform into even more disbursed, nimble organizations out of necessity."[26]

The purpose of journalism is not defined by technology. It is "the enterprise—journalism—that gives technology purpose, shape, perspective, meaning and significance," not the other way around.[27] The core identities of journalism are not so much about technological bells and whistles as going to places, knocking on doors, and talking to people whom journalism purports to serve. Scholars and practitioners of journalism need to go back to the basics and think about what journalism is and why journalism matters to society. While technology evolves fast, journalism needs to go slow, considering the roles it plays in people's lives.

Notes

Introduction

1. Branch, "Snow Fall." For interviews with the creators, see Duenes et al., "How We Made Snow Fall"; see also Dowling and Vogan, "Can We 'Snowfall' This?"

2. Greenfield, "What the New York Times's 'Snow Fall' Means."

3. Dowling and Vogan, "Can We 'Snowfall' This?," 6.

4. Manjoo, "Whole Lot of Bells," par. 5.

5. Posetti, *Time to Step Away*, 7.

6. For a general overview of slow journalism, see David, Blumtritt, and Köhler, "Slow Media Manifesto," and Le Masurier, "What Is Slow Journalism?"

7. Kline, "Technological Determinism," 109.

8. McLuhan, *Gutenberg Galaxy*. Disputes exist about whether McLuhan indeed believed in technological determinism. Some argue that his views cannot be easily reduced to technological determinism, and that even if he was a determinist, he endorsed a lighter version of it, believing that while the use of particular media may have subtle influences on humans, it is the social context of use that is also crucial. For further discussion, see Ralon, "Beyond Categorization." However, many observers, especially outside academia, consider him as a technological evangelist who foresaw the enormous power of new media technologies.

9. Tarr, Finholt, and Goodman, "City and the Telegraph."

10. Chandler, *Visible Hand*.

11. See, for example, Fulk, "Social Construction of Communication Technology," and MacKenzie and Wajcman, *Social Shaping of Technology*.

12. Williams, *Television*, 133. It is important to note that Williams was also critical of an extreme version of social construction of technology. In the same passage, he subsequently said the notion of a socially determined technology has "a similar one-sided, one-way version of human process" as technological determinism.

13. Diamond, *Guns, Germs, and Steel*, chapter 3. Diamond emphasizes that the colonizers' gun technology was instrumental in the defeat of Native Americans. But he also makes an argument that a series of other factors, including geography, epidemics, and the blunders of Native American leaders, contributed to their quick demise at the hands of Spanish soldiers.

14. A good edited volume on this subject is Smith and Marx, *Does Technology Drive History?*

15. Kline and Kline, *Consumers in the Country*, 10.

16. See the historical arguments from Pinch and Bijker, "Social Construction of Facts."

17. Dafoe, "On Technological Determinism," 1050.

18. It is said that he made this remark to his colleagues sometime during the 1960s or '70s. It is not clear exactly when he said it and in what context. See Ridley, "Don't Write Off the Next Big Thing."

19. Krugman, "Why Most Economists' Predictions Are Wrong."

20. See, for example, Dedehayir and Steinert, "Hype Cycle Model," and the Gartner Research page on hype cycles available at https://www.gartner.com/en/research/methodologies/gartner-hype-cycle. In communication studies and sociology, the classic diffusion of innovation theory suggests that people's adoption of innovation takes place in stages—from early adopters to laggards. See Rogers, *Diffusion of Innovation*.

21. Misa, "How Machines Make History," 308.

22. Ellul, *Technological System*. Ellul argues that technology constitutes a "system" of which humans are a part, where all human choices are made within the bounds set by technology.

23. Misa, "How Machines Make History," 320.

24. DeSanctis and Poole, "Capturing the Complexity."

25. For a good account of the decision school, see Perrow, *Complex Organizations*.

26. Orlikowski, "Duality of Technology."

27. Misa, "How Machines Make History," 320.

28. Giddens, *Constitution of Society*, 376.

29. See, for example, Avilés et al., "Journalists at Digital Television Newsrooms"; Huang et al., "Facing the Challenges of Convergence"; and Quinn, *Conversations on Convergence*.

30. See, for example, McNair, *Sociology of Journalism*; Negroponte, *Being Digital*; and Pavlik, "Impact of Technology."

31. Some notable works include Barnhurst and Nerone, *Form of News*; Boczkowski, "Processes of Adopting Multimedia"; Dooley, *Technology of Journalism*; Örnebring, "Technology and Journalism-as-Labour"; Spyridou et al., "Journalism in a State"; and Schreiber and Zimmermann, *Journalism and Technological Change*.

32. Mari, *Short History*.

33. Boczkowski, "Processes of Adopting Multimedia," 201.

Chapter 1

1. See, for example, Pavlik, *Journalism and New Media*, and McNair, *Sociology of Journalism*.

2. McNair, *Sociology of Journalism*, 125.

3. Dooley, *Technology of Journalism*, 140.

4. This chapter does not specifically discuss two dominant journalism technologies of recent years—data journalism and social media. This is because data journalism is more of a set of practices rather than material technology, and social media can be considered part of the internet. Considering their contemporary significance, however, these technologies and technology-supported practices are discussed more in depth in the conclusion.

5. For a failed technology like videotex, see Picard, "Changing Business Models."

6. Some notable works in this regard include Anderson, *Imagined Communities*; Davis, *Lost Gutenberg*; Eisenstein, *Printing Press*; Man, *Gutenberg Revolution*; McLuhan, *Gutenberg Galaxy*; and McMurtrie, *Book*.

7. Eisenstein, *Printing Press*, 704.

8. Weber, "Strassburg."

9. The World Association of Newspapers (WAN) accepted the evidence from the Gutenberg Museum in Mainz, Germany, that the "birth certificate" of the newspaper, *Relation*, was unearthed in the town archives of Strasbourg. See the archived version of the WAN's website at https://web.archive.org/web/20100310235015/http://www.wan-press.org/article6476.html. See also Weber, "Strassburg." There are disputes over this claim, however. Most notably, the Chinese had been publishing newspapers since ancient times. But their irregularity and official nature may not qualify them as "modern" newspapers.

10. Pettegree, *Invention of News*, chapter 9. See also Stephens, *History of News*, part 4.

11. For a good overview of the printing press technology in East Asia, see Tsien, *Science and Civilisation in China*. See also Christensen, *River of Ink*, and Gunaratne, "Paper, Printing and the Printing Press."

12. Tsien, *Science and Civilisation in China*.

13. Eisenstein, *Printing Press*, 23.

14. Hanqi, *History of Journalism in China*.

15. Tsien, *Science and Civilisation in China*, 382–83.

16. Febvre and Martin, *Coming of the Book*.

17. Still, many scholars acknowledge Gutenberg as the inventor of the printing press. Not many historical records exist about the inventors before him.

18. Dooley, *Technology of Journalism*, chapter 2.

19. Pettegree, *Invention of News*, 6.

20. Ibid., 372.

21. For a good overview of early printing in America, see Blumenthal, *Printed Book in America*.

22. Massachusetts governor Simon Bradstreet issued the following order on September 29, 1690:

WHEREAS some have lately presumed to Print and Disperse a Pamphlet, (Entituled, Publick Occurrences, both Forreign and Domestick: Boston, Thursday, Septemb. 25th. 1690). Without the least Privity or Countenance of Authority. The Governour and Council having had the perusal of the said Pamphlet, and finding that therein is contained Reflections of a very high nature: As also sundry doubtful and uncertain Reports, do hereby manifest and declare their high Resentment and Disallowance of said Pamphlet, and Order that the same be Suppressed and called in; strictly forbidding any person or persons for the future to Set forth anything in Print without Licence first obtained from those that are or shall be appointed by the Government to grant the same.

See Moody and Simmons, *Glorious Revolutions in Massachusetts*, 275. See also Sloan, "Chaos, Polemics."

23. Professional practices in the New York bar different from those of earlier courts included the use of a writ and more witnesses in trials. See Moglen, "Considering Zenger," and Rosen, "Supreme Court of Judicature."

24. Carey, *Communication as Culture*, 304.

25. Many historians and media scholars as well as journalists endorse this view. See, for example, Scanlan, "Birth of the Inverted Pyramid"; Porwancher, "Objectivity's Prophet"; and Stephens, *History of News*.

26. Rogers, *Communication Technology*, 30.

27. Errico et al., "Evolution of the Summary News Lead."

28. Pöttker, "News and Its Communicative Quality."

29. Stensaas, "Objective News Report."

30. For a copy of the original reporting, see "AP Was There."

31. Errico et al., "Evolution of the Summary News Lead."

32. Pöttker, "News and Its Communicative Quality," 510.

33. Mindich, *Just the Facts*, chapter 3.

34. This is especially the case for French journalism. See Chalaby, "Journalism as an Anglo-American Invention."

35. Mari, *Short History*.

36. While OCR and videotex were short lived, VDTs were more successful and they were an important precursor to personal, desktop computers.

37. Kirschenbaum, *Track Changes*, xi.

38. Mari, *Short History*, 158 (e-book version).

39. Ibid., 33.

40. Locke, "Telecommunication in the News Industry," 290.

41. Ibid., 284.

42. Mari, *Short History*, 75–76 (e-book version).

43. Wilken, "Behavioral Dynamics Stressed," 22.

44. See, for example, Aronson, Sylvie, and Todd, "Real-Time Journalism"; Garrison, "Diffusion of Online Information"; and Russial, "Pagination and the Newsroom."

45. Boczkowski, "Processes of Adopting Multimedia," 198.

46. For early utopian accounts of the internet, see, for example, Grossman, *Electronic Republic*, and Rheingold, *Virtual Community*. At the other end of the spectrum, for accounts of the internet being less transformative, see Margolis and Resnick, *Politics as Usual*, and Wilhelm, *Democracy in the Digital Age*.

47. "Newspapers Fact Sheet."

48. "Employment Trends in Newspaper Publishing."

49. The statistics through 2014 come from *Editor and Publisher*. The numbers for 2015 and afterward are estimates based on Pew Research Center analysis of Alliance for Audited Media data. For more on the Pew research methodology, see "Newspapers Fact Sheet."

50. Data drawn from the World Press Trends Database, available at http://www.wptdatabase.org/.

51. This is a main thesis of the two books by Robert McChesney. See McChesney, *Rich*

Media, Poor Democracy, and McChesney and Nichols, *Death and Life*.

52. Fenton, *Bad News*. In the 1990s, TV news shows such as *Dateline* began to air, largely producing low-quality crime stories, usually on weekends.

53. US Senate, *Future of Journalism*.

54. With the death of George Floyd by the hands of the police in Minnesota and ensuing protests worldwide, the year 2020 seems to be the apex of Black Lives Matter. However, the movement began in July 2013 on Twitter when the #BlackLivesMatter hashtag began to appear after the acquittal of George Zimmerman, who in February 2012 shot and killed Trayvon Martin, an African American teen.

55. See, for example, DeLuca, Lawson, and Sun, "Occupy Wall Street on the Public," and Min, "Occupy Wall Street and Deliberative."

56. Weinberger, "Transparency Is the New Objectivity."

57. "Code of Ethics." It was revised in 2014 to include a section titled "Be Accountable and Transparent."

58. Singer, "Political J-Blogger," 179.

59. Ibid., 189.

60. Lasorsa, Lewis, and Holton, "Normalizing Twitter."

61. "Public Trust in Government."

62. Min, *As Democracy Goes*, chapter 4.

63. Ibid., 75.

64. Andersen, "How America Lost Its Mind," 80.

65. For the interactive online story, see "Apollo 11 Moon Landing." For details on how the *Times* produced the story, see Roberts and Corum, "How We Augmented Our Original Reporting."

66. Taddonio, "After Solitary."

67. Milk, "How Virtual Reality Can Create."

68. Archer and Finger, "Walking in Another's Virtual Shoes"; Kang et al., "Immersive Journalism and Telepresence"; Laws, "Can Immersive Journalism Enhance Empathy?"

69. Goldman Sachs Group, *Virtual and Augmented Reality*, 7.

70. De la Peña et al., "Immersive Journalism."

71. Hassan, "Digitality, Virtual Reality," 192.

72. Ibid., 192.

73. For a good review of the ethical issues concerning VR/AR, see Madary and Metzinger, "Real Virtuality."

74. For detailed accounts and analysis, see English, "Political Photography," and Przyblyski, "Revolution at a Standstill."

75. Kent, "Ethical Reality Check."

76. MBC, South Korea's top broadcaster, produced the story. Watch the documentary at https://www.youtube.com/watch?v=uflTK8c4w0c&t=43s. For more discussion of the event, see Kim, "Virtual Reality, Real Grief."

77. VR news entrepreneurs interviewed in Watson, *VR for News*, consider branded content a viable option.

78. See, for example, Boden, *AI*; Ekbia, *Artificial Dreams*; and Marcus and Davis, *Rebooting AI*.

79. Martin, "Myth of the Awesome Thinking Machine," 122.

80. Natale and Ballatore, "Imagining the Thinking Machine," 4.

81. Newquist, *Brain Makers*.

82. Interview with an anonymous data scientist, featured in *Logic* magazine: "The Smart, the Stupid, and the Catastrophically Scary."

83. See Diakopoulos, *Automating the News*, chapter 1.

84. Hamilton, *Democracy's Detectives*, chapters 1 and 8.

85. Diakopoulos, "Artificial Intelligence–Enhanced Journalism."

86. See, for example, Bakshy, Messing, and Adamic, "Exposure to Ideologically Diverse News"; Barnidge, "Exposure to Political Disagreement"; Gentzkow and Shapiro, "Ideological Segregation Online and Offline"; Haim, Graefe, and Brosius, "Burst of the Filter Bubble?"; Min and Wohn, "All the News"; and Min and Wohn, "Underneath the Filter Bubble."

87. For a detailed argument on this, see my earlier work, Min, *As Democracy Goes*, chapter 5.

88. Belair-Gagnon, Lewis, and Agur, "Failure to Launch," 299.

89. DeSanctis and Poole, "Capturing the Complexity."

90. Belair-Gagnon, Lewis, and Agur, "Failure to Launch," 300.

91. Ivancsics, "Blockchain in Journalism," 10.

92. See "Trust Machine."

93. For more details, see Ingram, "Civil Primer," and Shilina, "Journalism + Blockchain."

94. Aiello, "As Hedge Funds Overtake Media."

95. Ryckman, "Colorado Sun Wins."

96. For the editor's statement on this, see Ryckman, "From the Editor."

97. Gerard, *Attack of the 50 Foot Blockchain*, 109.

98. To read about how the company stopped operation, see Kasireddy, "Why TruStory Is Shutting Down."

99. For an interview with Reddit's general manager, Eric Martin, discussing many of these issues, see Spinks, "Distributed Control."

100. Herian, "Politics of Blockchain," 166.

101. Swartz, "Blockchain Dreams," 99.

102. Barnhurst and Nerone, *Form of News*, 8.

103. Mari, *Short History*, 24 (e-book version).

104. For a good overview of the relationship between journalism and public life, see Ryfe, *Journalism and the Public*.

105. Dooley, *Technology of Journalism*, 16.

Chapter 2

1. Royal, "Are Journalism Schools Teaching?"

2. To access the full leaked report, see Abbruzzese, "Full New York Times Innovation Report."

3. Usher, *Making News*.

4. Benson and Neveu, *Bourdieu and the Journalistic Field*; Benson, "Field Theory in Comparative Context"; Bourdieu, *On Television and Journalism*.

5. Bourdieu and Wacquant, *Invitation to Reflexive Sociology*, 97.

6. Benson and Neveu, *Bourdieu and the Journalistic Field*, 3.

7. Bourdieu and Wacquant, *Invitation to Reflexive Sociology*, 126.

8. Benson and Neveu, *Bourdieu and the Journalistic Field*, 3.

9. Some classic sociological studies include Carr-Saunders and Wilson, *Professions*, and Larson, *Rise of Professionalism*.

10. Schudson and Anderson, "Objectivity, Professionalism, and Truth Seeking."

11. Collins and Evans, *Rethinking Expertise*, 35.

12. A representative work in this regard is Abbott, *System of Professions*.

13. Usher, *Interactive Journalism*, chapter 1.

14. Waisbord, *Reinventing Professionalism*.

15. Benson and Neveu, *Bourdieu and the Journalistic Field*, 4.

16. Witschge and Nygren, "Journalistic Work," 56.

17. Tandoc, "Journalism Is Twerking?," 4.

18. Wu, Tandoc, and Salmon, "Field Analysis of Journalism," 437.

19. Usher, *Interactive Journalism*.

20. Ibid., 41.

21. Benson and Neveu, *Bourdieu and the Journalistic Field*, 6.

22. Lowrey, "Routine News"; Lowrey, "Normative Conflict in the Newsroom."

23. Benson, "Field Theory in Comparative Context," 468.

24. Vos and Craft, "Discursive Construction of Journalistic Transparency," 1505–6.

25. Zelizer, *Taking Journalism Seriously*, chapter 7.

26. Vos and Perreault, "Discursive Construction of the Gamification," 473.

27. New York Times, *Innovation*, 61, the leaked version of which is accessible via Abbruzzese, "Full New York Times Innovation Report."

28. Ibid., 25.

29. Ibid., 31.

30. Carlson, "Metajournalistic Discourse," 350.

31. Creech and Nadler, "Post-Industrial Fog," 186.

32. See, for example, Ferrucci, Nelson, and Davis, "From 'Public Journalism' to 'Engaged Journalism'"; Powers, "'In Forms That Are Familiar'"; and Vos and Singer, "Media Discourse About Entrepreneurial Journalism."

33. Powers, "'In Forms That Are Familiar.'"

34. Since *American Journalism Review* ceased publication in 2015, the data from this publication contain articles in or prior to 2015; only magazine articles, not blog posts, were analyzed for *Columbia Journalism Review*.

35. Corbin and Strauss, *Basics of Qualitative Research*; Emerson, Fretz, and Shaw, *Writing Ethnographic Fieldnotes*; Glaser and Strauss, *Discovery of Grounded Theory*.

36. Charmaz, "Qualitative Interviewing," 675.

37. Powers, "'In Forms That Are Familiar,'" 34.

38. Mutter, "Big Data Is a Big Deal," 20.

39. Young, "News on the Dash," 8.

40. Stray, "Age of the Cyborg."

41. Stepp, "Maybe It Is Time to Panic," 22.

42. "Letter from the Staff: A New Year's Wish from B&C."

43. "Letter from the Staff: OK, We Can Do This."

44. Powers, "'In Forms That Are Familiar,'" 30.

45. This is a quote from Jeremy Gilbert, *Washington Post* director of strategic initiatives; see Stroh, "Artificial World," 34–35.

46. Suciu, "New Perception," 40.

47. Gallagher, "Editor Is Not an Algorithm," 22.

48. Gilbert, "AI Finally Becomes Helpful."

49. Smolkin, "Adapt or Die."

50. Schudson, "Objectivity Norm in American Journalism." Schudson argues that the objectivity norm emerged in the late nineteenth and early twentieth centuries as an instance of a general social phenomenon. The norm was discursively constituted to satisfy the need to articulate the ideals of social practice in a group in order to exercise control over subordinates and to pass on group culture to the next generation.

51. Vos and Craft, "Discursive Construction of Journalistic Transparency," 1505.

52. Powers, "'In Forms That Are Familiar,'" 36–37.

53. "Carnegie-Knight Initiative."

54. Job advertisement 30882BR—Job Title Reporter / Video Journalist for NBC News Studio, 2017.

55. The sampling frame was IRE professional members who joined the group sometime between 2018 and 2020. A total of 4,462 people were contacted; 226 people completed the survey and 163 partially finished it, yielding a response rate of 8.7 percent (based on RR4 in American Association for Public Opinion Research). This figure mirrors the general trend of falling response rates among surveys of journalists. See Molyneux, Lewis, and Holton, "Media Work, Identity"; Örnebring and Mellado, "Valued Skills among Journalists"; and Zamith, Belair-Gagnon, and Lewis, "Constructing Audience Quantification." The final sample was 48 percent male and 52 percent female; in terms of race and ethnicity, it was 82.4 percent white, 6.3 percent Hispanic, 2.7 percent Black, 4.5 percent Asian or Pacific Islander, 0.5 percent Native American, and 3.6 percent categorized as other. About 98 percent of the sample had a college or higher degree, and their median work experience was between eleven and twenty years. The vast majority of the journalists (72.3 percent) had a journalism-related degree. About half (50.1 percent) identified as reporters, 16 percent as editors, 6.2 percent as producers, 5.3 percent as managers, and the rest (22.4 percent) as other. Newspaper journalists were the most numerous at about 26 percent, followed by digital/internet only (20 percent), TV (17 percent), radio (15 percent), magazine (6.7 percent), wire service (4.3 percent), and freelance/other (11 percent).

56. Örnebring, "Technology and Journalism-as-Labour," 64.

57. Petre, "Engineering Consent," 510.

58. Creech and Mendelson, "Imagining the Journalist of the Future," 148.

59. Ibid., 144.

60. Avilés et al., "Journalists at Digital Television Newsrooms."

61. Liu, "De-skilling Effects on Journalists."

62. These digital and traditional skills are not necessarily mutually exclusive. For example, source development and fact-checking may very well happen on social media and can be considered part of digital skills. However, an analysis of the data suggests there are clearly two factors in the answers—digital versus traditional—at least in the perception of these reporters.

63. Zelizer, "Why Journalism Is About More," 345.

64. Powers, "New Boots on the Ground."

65. Min, *As Democracy Goes*, chapter 4.

66. Faber and McCarthy, *Foundations for Social Change*, part 1.

67. Woo, "As Old Gods Falter."

68. Lewis, "From Journalism to Information," 310.

69. Ibid., 315.

70. Creech and Nadler, "Post-Industrial Fog," 189.

71. Tandoc and Maitra, "News Organizations' Use," 1685.

72. Kamenetz, "How Upworthy Used Emotional Data."

73. Sanders, "Upworthy Was One of the Hottest Sites Ever."

74. Dick, "Search Engine Optimisation in UK."

75. Tandoc and Maitra, "News Organizations' Use."

76. Rashidian et al., *Friend and Foe.*

77. This is more the case for powerful players in journalism. Small and midsized newsrooms still heavily depend on third-party tools and resources.

78. Doctor, "Newsonomics."

79. Fanta, "Publisher's Patron."

80. Bell, "Do Technology Companies Care About Journalism?"

81. See, for example, Avilés et al., "Journalists at Digital Television Newsrooms," and Huang et al., "Facing the Challenges of Convergence."

82. Creech and Mendelson, "Imagining the Journalist of the Future," 143.

83. Marjoribanks, "'Anti-Wapping'?"; Örnebring, "Technology and Journalism-as-Labour." For a general thesis about the subordination of technology to capitalism, see Braverman, *Labor and Monopoly Capital.*

Chapter 3

1. Feola, "State of Denial for Newspapers."

2. For general arguments for slow life, see Parkins and Craig, *Slow Living.*

3. The slow food manifesto is available from the nonprofit organization Slow Food at https://www.slowfood.com/about-us/our -philosophy.

4. Sabria, Blumtritt, and Köhler, "Slow Media Manifesto." See also Laufer, *Slow News,* and Rauch, *Slow Media.*

5. Mindfulness has always been a central concept in Buddhist philosophy; Nietzsche mentioned slow reading in his 1881 work *The Dawn of Day.* In the preface of the latter, Nietzsche wrote:

I have not been a philologist in vain—perhaps I am one yet: a teacher of slow reading. I even come to write slowly. At present it is not only my habit, but even my taste—a perverted taste, maybe—to write nothing but what will drive to despair everyone who is "in a hurry." For philology is that venerable art which exacts from its followers one thing above all—to step to one side, to leave themselves spare moments, to grow silent, to become slow—the leisurely art of the goldsmith applied to language: an art which must carry out slow, fine work, and attains nothing if not *lento.* (13–14)

6. Goodman, "Transcendentalism."

7. Rauch, *Slow Media,* 1–2.

8. Edwards, *Sustainability Revolution.*

9. Abe, *Zen and Comparative Studies,* 163.

10. Ibid., 164–66. See also Galtung, *Peace by Peaceful Means.* In Christianity, you overcome your sinful time in the secular world and enter the Kingdom of God upon death. In Buddhism, you emancipate yourself from the infinite cycles of birth, life, and death through the attainment of nirvana.

11. Abe, *Zen and Comparative Studies,* 164.

12. Hanh, *Miracle of Mindfulness,* 30.

13. Le Masurier, "What Is Slow Journalism?," 148.

14. Ibid., 149.

15. Ambroise, "Fast but Slow," 84.

16. Even in the case of the sixteenth-century Luddites, an argument can be made that they were not necessarily anti-technology. Kevin Binfield suggests that the Luddites were totally fine with machines—they just wanted these machines to be run by workers who had gone through an apprenticeship and got paid decent wages. In other words, Luddism was more a case of labor disputes against the social conditions that subjected workers to what they saw as unfair treatment. See Binfield, *Writings of the Luddites.*

17. Rauch, *Slow Media,* chapter 6.

18. Ibid., 116.

19. Parkins and Craig, *Slow Living,* ix.

20. Gess, "Climate Change."

21. Rauch, *Slow Media,* chapter 3.

22. Gunaratne, "Buddhist Goals of Journalism."

23. For a detailed discussion of mindful journalism, see Gunaratne, Pearson, and Senarath, *Mindful Journalism.*

24. Despite the slow journalism mission, *Delayed Gratification* maintains a useful website at https://www.slow-journalism.com/.

25. See https://decorrespondent.nl. See also Le Masurier, "What Is Slow Journalism?" The American version, the *Correspondent*, unfortunately ceased operation in January 2021 due to financial setbacks.

26. Carretero and Bariain, "Slow Journalism in Spain," 528.

27. Drok and Hermans, "Is There a Future?," 542.

28. Min, *As Democracy Goes*, chapter 2.

29. Anderson, Dardenne, and Killenberg, *Conversation of Journalism*, chapter 3.

30. Rauch, *Slow Media*, 36.

31. Örnebring, "Technology and Journalism-as-Labor," 65. See also Hampton, *Visions of the Press*.

32. Gans, *Democracy and the News*, 50.

33. Drok and Hermans, "Is There a Future?," 540.

34. For good arguments about how speed comes at the cost of good reporting, see Laufer, *Slow News*, and Rosenberg and Feldman, *No Time to Think*.

35. Kang, "Should Reddit Be Blamed." See also the documentary film *Help Us Find Sunil Tripathi*, which documents the collective fear, group mentality, and media frenzy that wrongfully implicated Sunil Tripathi, a university student who disappeared from his apartment, in the Boston Marathon bombings.

36. Welsh, "Did the Media Botch the Boston Bombing?"

37. Fuchs, "Jumping to Conclusions."

38. Watch the *CBS Evening News*, April 19, 1995, at https://www.youtube.com/watch?time_continue=37&v=lU3Cfal3xN0; the *Wall Street Journal* phrase is quoted in Fuchs, "Jumping to Conclusions" (the original *Journal* article appears to have been removed from the newspaper's online archive).

39. Craig, "Reclaiming Slowness in Journalism," 463.

40. Min, "Conversation Through Journalism," 568–69.

41. Min, *As Democracy Goes*, chapter 3.

42. Wenzel, Gerson, and Moreno, "Engaging Communities Through Solutions Journalism."

43. McIntyre and Gyldensted, "Constructive Journalism," 21.

44. For a good review of engaged journalism, see Lawrence, Radcliffe, and Schmidt, "Practicing Engagement"; Min, "What the Twenty-First Century"; and Nelson, "And Deliver Us to Segmentation."

45. This popular business term comes from Bower and Christensen, "Disruptive Technologies." While this concept has been celebrated in business, its empirical basis is rather shaky, and it has been used too loosely for many different contexts. For criticism of the concept, see Markides, "Disruptive Innovation," and Vázquez Sampere, Bienenstock, and Zuckerman, "Debating Disruptive Innovation."

46. The overall failure rate of start-ups is estimated at 90 percent. See Griffith, "Why Startups Fail"; see also Luo and Mann, "Survival and Growth."

47. Examples include companies like Uber and Snapchat. These companies have been barely profitable, but their utmost priority is to expand their userbases quickly. Facebook and Amazon adopted similar strategies during their early years. For more discussion, see Holmes, "From Snap to Uber."

48. Küng, *Going Digital*, 13.

49. A vast majority of journalists interviewed by Posetti for the report *Time to Step Away* expressed such a feeling.

50. Creech and Nadler, "Post-Industrial Fog," 191.

51. Kabat-Zinn, "Mindfulness-Based Interventions," 56.

52. Pearson, McMahon, and O'Donovan, "Potential Benefits of Teaching Mindfulness."

53. Meyer, *Vanishing Newspaper*.

54. For more discussion, see Porter, *Competitive Advantage*.

55. Meyer, *Vanishing Newspaper*, 212–13.

56. Bruns, "Media Innovations, User Innovations," 14.

57. Senarath, "Journalism and the Middle Path," 140.

58. Sylvie and Witherspoon, *Time, Change*, chapter 7.

59. See *BuzzFeed*'s YouGov survey standing at https://today.yougov.com/topics/media/explore/website/Buzzfeed. See also Saba, "Beyond Cute Cats."

60. Blake et al., "From Russia with Blood."

61. Hamby, "Inside the Global 'Club.'"

62. Kenneally, "We Saw Nuns Kill Children."

63. Küng, *Innovators in Digital News*, 58.

64. The *BuzzFeed* team has produced fascinating data journalism stories using sophisticated algorithms. For example, they trained a computer to search for hidden spy planes in the sky. In another instance, they analyzed tennis-match data and found that some contests were fixed due to influence from organized criminal groups. See Heidi and Templon, "Tennis Racket," and Aldhous, "Here's How Buzzfeed News."

65. Küng, *Innovators in Digital News*, 72.

66. Tandoc, "Five Ways BuzzFeed Is Preserving," 211.

67. Stringer, "Finding a Place," 1994–95.

68. Tandoc, "Five Ways BuzzFeed Is Preserving," 211.

69. Google Analytics data from January 2019, as reported in the *Guardian* media kit; available at https://advertising.theguardian.com/advertising/media-kit.

70. See, for example, Marchi, *Self-Reflexive Journalism*; Chadwick and Collister, "Boundary-Drawing Power"; and Pavlik, "Innovation and the Future."

71. Küng, *Innovators in Digital News*, chapter 2.

72. See, for example, Bruns, "Media Innovations, User Innovations"; Kane et al., *Technology Fallacy*; Küng, *Innovators in Digital News*; and Porcu, "Exploring Innovative Learning Culture."

73. DeSanctis and Poole, "Capturing the Complexity." See also Orlikowski, "Using Technology and Constituting Structures."

74. This figure was inspired from the "Journalism Innovation Wheel," developed from the Journalism Innovation Project at the Reuters Institute for the Study of Journalism. See Posetti, *Time to Step Away*, 14.

75. Küng, *Innovators in Digital News*.

76. Some examples include Lewis, "Tension Between Professional Control"; Ryfe, *Can Journalism Survive?*; and Usher, *Making News*.

77. Gade, "Newspapers and Organizational Development."

78. Kanter, Stein, and Jick, *Challenge of Organizational Change*.

79. Kane et al., *Technology Fallacy*.

80. Sylvie and Witherspoon, *Time, Change*, chapter 7.

81. Ibid., 194.

82. Küng, *Innovators in Digital News*, chapter 2.

83. Wenger, McDermott, and Snyder, *Cultivating Communities of Practice*.

84. Porcu, "Exploring Innovative Learning," 1568.

85. Ekdale et al., "Making Change."

86. Lajqi and Lischka, "Normative Principles in Newsroom Innovation."

87. Domingo, "Interactivity in the Daily Routines." Similar results can be found from the following studies: Lasorsa, Lewis, and Holton, "Normalizing Twitter"; Spyridou et al., "Journalism in a State of Flux"; and Steensen, "What's Stopping Them?"

88. Lehtisaari et al., "Comparing Innovation," 1031.

89. Sylvie and Witherspoon, *Time, Change*, chapter 7.

90. Küng, *Innovators in Digital News*, 25–26.

91. Peters, "Web Focus Helps."

92. Geiß, Jackob, and Quiring, "Impact of Communicating Digital Technologies," 1059.

93. Zahra and George, "Absorptive Capacity."

94. Sylvie and Witherspoon, *Time, Change*, chapter 7.

95. Gade and Perry, "Changing the Newsroom Culture."

96. Nip, "Last Days of Civic Journalism."

97. Sylvie and Witherspoon, *Time, Change*, 187.

98. Lichterman, "How Germany's Die Zeit"; Schantin, "Innovation Matters."

99. Peterson, "At the New Yorker Festival."

100. Lawrence et al., *Building Engagement*, 35.

101. Ibid., 31.

102. Israel, "On the Table."

103. Lawrence et al., *Building Engagement*, 8.

104. These offline, in-person activities were gaining momentum just before the COVID-19 pandemic hit in early 2020. The pandemic stopped almost all of newsrooms' in-person audience engagement efforts. It may also have permanently altered how people interact, such that people have become more receptive to virtual gatherings. At the same time, people's desire to be in contact with other human beings and be sociable is growing during the quarantine caused by the

pandemic. The future trend of audience engagement will likely be some form of mixed efforts accommodating both virtual and in-person activities.

105. Posetti, Simon, and Shabbir, *What If Scale Breaks Community?*

106. Ibid., 47.

107. Örnebring, "Technology and Journalism-as-Labour," 65.

Conclusion

1. See Stevens, "Why Outbreaks Like Coronavirus Spread."

2. Mukherjee, "How Does the Coronavirus Behave Inside a Patient?," emphasis in original.

3. The past years have produced a series of works on how data and algorithms are influenced by sociocultural and political processes of society. Some notable examples include boyd and Crawford, "Critical Questions for Big Data"; Broussard, *Artificial Unintelligence*; Noble, *Algorithms of Oppression*; O'Neil, *Weapons of Math Destruction*; and Pasquale, *Black Box Society*.

4. Tong and Zuo, "Inapplicability of Objectivity," 6.

5. Some notable exceptions include data-driven investigative work conducted by such nonprofit news organizations as ProPublica and Reveal.

6. For the role of social media in the Arab Spring, see Hermida, *Tell Everyone*, and Khondker, "Role of the New Media."

7. Hermida, Lewis, and Zamith, "Sourcing the Arab Spring."

8. Lewis and Molyneux, "Decade of Research," 11. This work is based on Lewis's personal communication with reporters.

9. Waisbord, "Trolling Journalists."

10. Byman, "After the Hope."

11. For detailed arguments about how political and social conditions came before technology in the case of the Arab Spring, see Curran, "Internet of History," and Wolfsfeld et al., "Social Media and the Arab Spring."

12. Lewis and Molyneux, "Decades of Research," 18.

13. Powers, "'In Forms That Are Familiar,'" 31.

14. Creech and Nadler, "Post-Industrial Fog," 183.

15. Örnebring, "Technology and Journalism-as-Labour," 65.

16. Weaver and Wu, *Global Journalist*, 468; see also Weaver and Willnat, *Global Journalist in the 21st Century*.

17. Classic works in journalism theories, too, have been criticized as displaying ethnocentric views. A prime example is the work by Siebert, Peterson, and Schramm, *Four Theories of the Press*, which critics saw as privileging a liberal Western model of the press. See also Christians et al., *Normative Theories of the Media*.

18. Schudson, *Why Journalism Still Matters*, chapter 1.

19. For a critical discussion of the relationship between journalism and democracy, see Josephi, "How Much Democracy"; Min, *As Democracy Goes*; and Zelizer, "On the Shelf Life of Democracy."

20. Ryfe, *Journalism and the Public*. The normative link between journalism and democracy is a well-explored idea. Empirically, however, journalism does not necessarily require democracy to operate. For example, some question whether an independent press requires a Western-style democratic government as a prerequisite, because quality journalism exists in nondemocratic countries, as shown in the case of Al Jazeera operating out of Qatar. See, for example, Josephi, "How Much Democracy."

21. Kovach and Rosenstiel, *Elements of Journalism*, 17.

22. Zelizer, "Why Journalism Is About More," 349. Some other journalism theorists endorse a similar view. See, for example, Meyer, *Vanishing Newspaper*, and Rosen, *What Are Journalists For?*

23. Westergaard and Jorgensen, "54 Newsrooms, 9 Countries." This comes from an English-language summary posted on the *Nieman Lab* blog. The original book was written in Danish in 2018 and no English translation has been made at this time of writing.

24. Creech and Nadler, "Post-Industrial Fog," 183–84.

25. Kovach and Rosenstiel, *Elements of Journalism*.

26. Mari, *Short History*, 160 (e-book version).

27. Zelizer, "Why Journalism Is About More," 349.

Bibliography

Abbott, Andrew. *The System of Professions: An Essay on the Division of Expert Labor.* Chicago: University of Chicago Press, 1988.

Abbruzzese, Jason. "The Full New York Times Innovation Report." *Mashable,* May 16, 2014. https://mashable.com /2014/05/16/full-new-york-times -innovation-report.

Abe, Masao. *Zen and Comparative Studies: Part Two of a Two-Volume Sequel to Zen and Western Thought.* Honolulu: University of Hawaii Press, 1997.

Aiello, Chloe. "As Hedge Funds Overtake Media, the *Denver Post* Leads a Vocal Revolt Against 'Vulture Capitalists.'" *CNBC,* June 16, 2018. https://www .cnbc.com/2018/06/16/denver-post -reporters-vs-vulture-capitalist- hedge-fund-alden.html.

Aldhous, Peter. "Here's How BuzzFeed News Trained a Computer to Search for Hidden Spy Planes." *BuzzFeed News,* August 7, 2017. https://www.buzzfeed news.com/article/peteraldhous/hidden -spy-planes.

Ambroise, Sofi. "Fast but Slow." *Slow* 4 (1997): 83–85.

Andersen, Kurt. "How America Lost Its Mind." *The Atlantic,* September 2017. https://www.theatlantic.com/maga zine/archive/2017/09/how-america -lost-its-mind/534231/.

Anderson, Benedict. *Imagined Communities: Reflections on the Origin and Spread of Nationalism.* New York: Verso, 1991.

Anderson, Rob, Robert Dardenne, and George Killenberg. *The Conversation of Journalism: Communication, Community, and News.* Westport, CT: Praeger, 1994.

"The Apollo 11 Moon Landing in Augmented Reality." *New York Times,* July 18, 2019. https://www.nytimes.com/inter active/2019/07/18/science/apollo-11 -moon-landing-photos-ul.html.

"AP Was There: Original AP Report of Lincoln's Assassination." Associated Press, April 13, 2015. https://apnews .com/91fed0359cc245f0960322a5e7 bac56a/ap-was-there-original-ap -report-lincolns-assassination.

Archer, Dan, and Katharina Finger. "Walking in Another's Virtual Shoes: Do 360- Degree Video News Stories Generate Empathy in Viewers?" *Columbia Journalism Review,* March 15, 2018. https://www.cjr.org/tow_center _reports/virtual-reality-news-empathy .php.

Aronson, Karla, George Sylvie, and Russell Todd. "Real-Time Journalism: Implications for News Writing." *Newspaper Research Journal* 17, nos. 3–4 (1996): 53–67. https://doi.org/10.1177/0739532 99601700305.

Avilés, José Alberto García, Bienvenido
León, Karen Sanders, and Jackie
Harrison. "Journalists at Digital
Television Newsrooms in Britain
and Spain: Workflow and Multi-
skilling in a Competitive Environment." *Journalism Studies* 5, no. 1
(2004): 87–100. https://doi.org/10
.1080/1461670032000174765.

Bakshy, Eytan, Solomon Messing, and
Lada A. Adamic. "Exposure to
Ideologically Diverse News and
Opinion on Facebook." *Science* 348,
no. 6239 (2015): 1130–32. https://doi
.org/10.1126/science.aaa1160.

Barnhurst, Kevin G., and John Nerone. *The
Form of News: A History*. New York:
Guilford Press, 2002.

Barnidge, Matthew. "Exposure to Political
Disagreement in Social Media Versus
Face-to-Face and Anonymous Online
Settings." *Political Communication* 34,
no. 2 (2017): 302–21. https://doi.org/10
.1080/10584609.2016.1235639.

Belair-Gagnon, Valerie, Seth C. Lewis, and
Colin Agur. "Failure to Launch:
Competing Institutional Logics,
Intrapreneurship, and the Case of
Chatbots." *Journal of Computer-
Mediated Communication* 25, no. 4
(2020): 291–306. https://doi.org/10
.1093/jcmc/zmaa008.

Bell, Emily. "Do Technology Companies
Care About Journalism?" *Columbia
Journalism Review*, March 27, 2019.
https://www.cjr.org/tow_center
/google-facebook-journalism-influ
ence.php.

Benson, Rodney. "Field Theory in Comparative Context: A New Paradigm for
Media Studies." *Theory and Society* 28,
no. 3 (1999): 463–98. https://doi.org
/10.1023/A:1006982529917.

Benson, Rodney, and Erik Neveu. *Bourdieu
and the Journalistic Field*. Malden, MA:
Polity, 2005.

Binfield, Kevin. *Writings of the Luddites*. Baltimore: Johns Hopkins University
Press, 2004.

Blake, Heidi, and John Templon. "The Tennis Racket." *BuzzFeed News*, January
17, 2016. https://www.buzzfeednews
.com/article/heidiblake/the-tennis
-racket.

Blake, Heidi, Tom Warren, Richard Holmes,
Jason Leopold, Jane Bradley, and
Alex Campbell. "From Russia With
Blood." *BuzzFeed*, June 15, 2017.
https://www.buzzfeed.com/heidiblake
/from-russia-with-blood-14-suspected
-hits-on-british-soil.

Blumenthal, Joseph. *The Printed Book in
America*. Lebanon, NH: University
Press of New England, 1989.

Boczkowski, Pablo J. "The Processes of
Adopting Multimedia and Interactivity in Three Online Newsrooms."
Journal of Communication 54, no. 2
(2004): 197–213. https://doi.org/10
.1111/j.1460-2466.2004.tb02624.x.

Boden, Margaret A. *AI: Its Nature and Future*.
New York: Oxford University Press,
2016.

Bourdieu, Pierre. *On Television and Journalism*.
Translated by Priscilla Ferguson. London: Pluto Press, 1998.

Bourdieu, Pierre, and Loïc J. D. Wacquant.
An Invitation to Reflexive Sociology.
Chicago: University of Chicago Press,
1992.

Bower, Joseph L., and Clayton M. Christensen. "Disruptive Technologies:
Catching the Wave." *Harvard Business
Review*, January 1, 1995. https://hbr
.org/1995/01/disruptive-technologies
-catching-the-wave.

boyd, danah, and Kate Crawford. "Critical
Questions for Big Data." *Information,
Communication and Society* 15, no. 5
(2012): 662–79. https://doi.org/10
.1080/1369118X.2012.678878.

Branch, John. "Snow Fall: The Avalanche at
Tunnel Creek." *New York Times*,
December 20, 2012. https://www
.nytimes.com/projects/2012/snow-fall/.

Braverman, Harry. *Labor and Monopoly Capi-
tal: The Degradation of Work in the
Twentieth Century*. New York: Monthly
Review Press, 1974.

Broussard, Meredith. *Artificial Unintelligence:
How Computers Misunderstand the
World*. Cambridge, MA: MIT Press,
2018.

Bruns, Axel. "Media Innovations, User
Innovations, Societal Innovations."
Journal of Media Innovations 1, no. 1
(2014): 13–27. https://doi.org/10.5617
/jmi.v1i1.827.

Byman, Daniel L. "After the Hope of the Arab Spring, the Chill of an Arab Winter." *Brookings Institute* (blog), December 4, 2011. https://www.brookings.edu/opinions/after-the-hope-of-the-arab-spring-the-chill-of-an-arab-winter.

Carey, James W. *Communication as Culture: Essays on Media and Society.* Boston: Unwin Hyman, 1989.

Carlson, Matt. "Metajournalistic Discourse and the Meanings of Journalism: Definitional Control, Boundary Work, and Legitimation." *Communication Theory* 26, no. 4 (2016): 349–68. https://doi.org/10.1111/comt.12088.

"Carnegie-Knight Initiative on the Future of Journalism Education." *Knight Foundation* (blog), February 10, 2011. https://knightfoundation.org/reports/carnegie-knight-initiative-future-journalism-educa.

Carretero, Alejandro Barranquero, and Garbiñe Jaurrieta Bariain. "Slow Journalism in Spain." *Journalism Practice* 10, no. 4 (2016): 521–38. https://doi.org/10.1080/17512786.2015.1124729.

Carr-Saunders, Sir Alexander Morris, and Paul Alexander Wilson. *The Professions.* Oxford: Clarendon Press, 1933.

Chadwick, Andrew, and Simon Collister. "Boundary-Drawing Power and the Renewal of Professional News Organizations: The Case of *The Guardian* and the Edward Snowden NSA Leak." *International Journal of Communication* 8 (2014): 2420–41.

Chalaby, Jean K. "Journalism as an Anglo-American Invention: A Comparison of the Development of French and Anglo-American Journalism, 1830s–1920s." *European Journal of Communication* 11, no. 3 (2016): 303–26. https://doi.org/10.1177/0267323196011003002.

Chandler, Alfred. *The Visible Hand: The Managerial Revolution in American Business.* Cambridge, MA: Harvard University Press, 1977.

Charmaz, Kathy. "Qualitative Interviewing and Grounded Theory Analysis." In *Handbook of Interview Research: Context and Method,* edited by Jaber Gubrium and James Holstein, 675–94. Thousand Oaks, CA: Sage, 2001.

Christensen, Thomas. *River of Ink: Literature, History, Art.* Berkeley, CA: Counterpoint Press, 2014.

Christians, Clifford G., Theodore Glasser, Denis McQuail, Kaarle Nordenstreng, and Robert A. White. *Normative Theories of the Media: Journalism in Democratic Societies.* Urbana: University of Illinois Press, 2009.

"Code of Ethics." *Society of Professional Journalists,* September 6, 2014. http://www.spj.org/ethicscode.asp.

Collins, Harry, and Robert Evans. *Rethinking Expertise.* Chicago: University of Chicago Press, 2007.

Corbin, Juliet, and Anselm Strauss. *Basics of Qualitative Research: Techniques and Procedures for Developing Grounded Theory.* Thousand Oaks, CA: Sage, 2014.

Craig, Geoffrey. "Reclaiming Slowness in Journalism." *Journalism Practice* 10, no. 4 (2016): 461–75. https://doi.org/10.1080/17512786.2015.1100521.

Creech, Brian, and Andrew L. Mendelson. "Imagining the Journalist of the Future: Technological Visions of Journalism Education and Newswork." *Communication Review* 18, no. 2 (2015): 142–65. https://doi.org/10.1080/10714421.2015.1031998.

Creech, Brian, and Anthony M. Nadler. "Post-Industrial Fog: Reconsidering Innovation in Visions of Journalism's Future." *Journalism* 19, no. 2 (2018): 182–99. https://doi.org/10.1177/1464884916689573.

Curran, James. "The Internet of History: Rethinking the Internet's Past." In *Misunderstanding the Internet,* edited by James Curran, Natalie Felton, and Des Freedman, 48–84. London: Routledge, 2016.

Dafoe, Allan. "On Technological Determinism: A Typology, Scope Conditions, and a Mechanism." *Science, Technology, and Human Values* 40, no. 6 (2015): 1047–76. https://doi.org/10.1177/0162243915579283.

David, Sabria, Jörg Blumtritt, and Benedikt Köhler. "Slow Media Manifesto." *Slow*

Media (blog), January 2, 2010. http://en.slow-media.net/manifesto.

Davis, Margaret Leslie. *The Lost Gutenberg: The Astounding Story of One Book's Five-Hundred-Year Odyssey*. New York: Penguin, 2019.

Dedehayir, Ozgur, and Martin Steinert. "The Hype Cycle Model: A Review and Future Directions." *Technological Forecasting and Social Change* 108 (2016): 28–41. https://doi.org/10.1016/j.techfore.2016.04.005.

De la Peña, Nonny, Peggy Weil, Joan Llobera, Bernhard Spanlang, Doron Friedman, Maria V. Sanchez-Vives, and Mel Slater. "Immersive Journalism: Immersive Virtual Reality for the First-Person Experience of News." *Presence: Teleoperators and Virtual Environments* 19, no. 4 (2010): 291–301. https://doi.org/10.1162/PRES_a_00005.

DeLuca, Kevin M., Sean Lawson, and Ye Sun. "Occupy Wall Street on the Public Screens of Social Media: The Many Framings of the Birth of a Protest Movement." *Communication, Culture and Critique* 5, no. 4 (2012): 483–509. https://doi.org/10.1111/j.1753-9137.2012.01141.x.

DeSanctis, Gerardine, and Marshall Scott Poole. "Capturing the Complexity in Advanced Technology Use: Adaptive Structuration Theory." *Organization Science* 5, no. 2 (1994): 121–47.

Diakopoulos, Nicholas. "Artificial Intelligence–Enhanced Journalism Offers a Glimpse of the Future of the Knowledge Economy." *Conversation*, June 11, 2019. http://theconversation.com/artificial-intelligence-enhanced-journalism-offers-a-glimpse-of-the-future-of-the-knowledge-economy-117728.

———. *Automating the News: How Algorithms Are Rewriting the Media*. Cambridge, MA: Harvard University Press, 2019.

Diamond, Jared M. *Guns, Germs, and Steel: The Fates of Human Societies*. New York: W. W. Norton, 1997.

Dick, Murray. "Search Engine Optimisation in UK News Production." *Journalism Practice* 5, no. 4 (2011): 462–77. https://doi.org/10.1080/17512786.2010.551020.

Doctor, Ken. "Newsonomics: The New York Times' New CEO, Meredith Levien, on Building a World-Class Digital Media Business—and a Tech Company." *Nieman Lab* (blog), July 30, 2020. https://www.niemanlab.org/2020/07/newsonomics-the-new-york-times-new-ceo-meredith-levien-on-building-a-world-class-digital-media-business-and-a-tech-company.

Domingo, David. "Interactivity in the Daily Routines of Online Newsrooms: Dealing with an Uncomfortable Myth." *Journal of Computer-Mediated Communication* 13, no. 3 (2008): 680–704. https://doi.org/10.1111/j.1083-6101.2008.00415.x.

Dooley, Patricia L. *The Technology of Journalism: Cultural Agents, Cultural Icons*. Evanston, IL: Northwestern University Press, 2007.

Dowling, David, and Travis Vogan. "Can We 'Snowfall' This?" *Digital Journalism* 3, no. 2 (2015): 209–24. https://doi.org/10.1080/21670811.2014.930250.

Drok, Nico, and Liesbeth Hermans. "Is There a Future for Slow Journalism?" *Journalism Practice* 10, no. 4 (2016): 539–54. https://doi.org/10.1080/17512786.2015.1102604.

Duenes, Steve, Eric Kissane, Andrew Kueneman, Jacky Myint, Graham Roberts, and Catherine Spangler. "How We Made Snow Fall." *Source* (blog), January 1, 2013. https://source.opennews.org/articles/how-we-made-snow-fall.

Edwards, Andres R. *The Sustainability Revolution: Portrait of a Paradigm Shift*. Gabriola Island, Canada: New Society, 2005.

Eisenstein, Elizabeth L. *The Printing Press as an Agent of Change*. Cambridge: Cambridge University Press, 1980.

Ekbia, H. R. *Artificial Dreams: The Quest for Non-Biological Intelligence*. New York: Cambridge University Press, 2008.

Ekdale, Brian, Jane B. Singer, Melissa Tully, and Shawn Harmsen. "Making Change: Diffusion of Technological, Relational, and Cultural Innovation in the Newsroom." *Journalism and Mass Communication Quarterly* 92, no. 4 (2015): 938–58. https://doi.org/10.1177/1077699015596337.

Ellul, Jacques. *The Technological System.* London: Continuum, 1980.

Emerson, Ralph Waldo. *Ralph Waldo Emerson.* New York: Oxford University Press, 1990.

Emerson, Robert M., Rachel I. Fretz, and Linda L. Shaw. *Writing Ethnographic Fieldnotes.* 2nd ed. Chicago: University of Chicago Press, 2011.

"Employment Trends in Newspaper Publishing and Other Media, 1990–2016." *US Bureau of Labor Statistics,* https://www .bls.gov/opub/ted/2016/employment -trends-in-newspaper-publishing-and -other-media-1990-2016.htm.

English, Donald E. "Political Photography and the Paris Commune of 1871: The Photographs of Eugène Appert." *History of Photography* 7, no. 1 (1983): 31–42. https://doi.org/10.1080/03087 298.1983.10442745.

Errico, Marcus, John April, Andrew Asch, Lynnette Khalfani, Miriam Smith, and Xochiti Ybarra. "The Evolution of the Summary News Lead." *Media History Monographs* 1, no. 1 (1997): 1–19.

Evans, Sandra K. "Making Sense of Innovation." *Journalism Studies* 19, no. 1 (2018): 4–24. https://doi.org/10.1080 /1461670X.2016.1154446.

Faber, Daniel, and Deborah McCarthy, eds. *Foundations for Social Change: Critical Perspectives on Philanthropy and Popular Movements.* Lanham, MD: Rowman and Littlefield, 2005.

Fanta, Alexander. "The Publisher's Patron: How Google's News Initiative Is Re-Defining Journalism." *European Journalism Observatory—EJO* (blog), September 26, 2018. https://en.ejo.ch/ digital-news/the-publishers-patron.

Febvre, Lucien, and Henri-Jean Martin. *The Coming of the Book: The Impact of Printing, 1450–1800.* Edited by Geoffrey Nowell-Smith and David Wootton. Translated by David Gerard. New York: Verso, 2010.

Fenton, Tom. *Bad News: The Decline of Reporting, the Business of News, and the Danger to Us All.* New York: Harper Collins, 2005.

Feola, C. "State of Denial for Newspapers." *Quill* 85 (1997): 28–29.

Ferrucci, Patrick, Jacob L. Nelson, and Miles P. Davis. "From 'Public Journalism' to 'Engaged Journalism': Imagined Audiences and Denigrating Discourse." *International Journal of Communication* 14 (2020): 1586–1604. https://ijoc.org/index.php/ijoc/article /view/11955/3010.

Fuchs, Penny Bender. "Jumping to Conclusions in Oklahoma City?" *American Journalism Review,* June 1995. https:// ajrarchive.org/Article.asp?id=1980&id =1980.

Fulk, Janet. "Social Construction of Communication Technology." *Academy of Management Journal* 36, no. 5 (1993): 921–50. https://doi.org/10.5465/256641.

Gaddis, John Lewis. *The Long Peace: Inquiries into the History of the Cold War.* New York: Oxford University Press, 1987.

Gade, Peter J. "Newspapers and Organizational Development: Management and Journalist Perceptions of Newsroom Cultural Change." *Journalism and Communication Monographs* 6, no. 1 (2004): 3–55. https://doi.org/10.1177 /152263790400600101.

Gade, Peter J., and Earnest L. Perry. "Changing the Newsroom Culture: A Four-Year Case Study of Organizational Development at the St. Louis Post-Dispatch." *Journalism and Mass Communication Quarterly* 80, no. 2 (2003): 327–47. https://doi.org/10.1177 /107769900308000207.

Gallagher, Tim. "An Editor Is Not an Algorithm." *Editor and Publisher* 151, no. 6 (June 2018): 22–23.

Galtung, Johan. *Peace by Peaceful Means: Peace and Conflict, Development and Civilization.* Thousand Oaks, CA: Sage, 1996.

Gans, Herbert J. *Democracy and the News.* New York: Oxford University Press, 2004.

Garrison, Bruce. "Diffusion of Online Information Technologies in Newspaper Newsrooms." *Journalism* 2, no. 2 (2001): 221–39. https://doi.org/10.1177 /146488490100200206.

Geiß, Stefan, Nikolaus Jackob, and Oliver Quiring. "The Impact of Communicating Digital Technologies: How Information and Communication Technology Journalists

Conceptualize Their Influence on the Audience and the Industry." *New Media and Society* 15, no. 7 (2013): 1058–76. https://doi.org/10.1177/1461 444812465597.

Gentzkow, Matthew, and Jesse M. Shapiro. "Ideological Segregation Online and Offline." *Quarterly Journal of Economics* 126, no. 4 (2011): 1799–1839. https://doi.org/10.1093/qje/qjr044.

Gerard, David. *Attack of the 50 Foot Blockchain: Bitcoin, Blockchain, Ethereum and Smart Contracts*. Self-published, CreateSpace, 2017.

Gess, Harold. "Climate Change and the Possibility of 'Slow Journalism.'" *Ecquid Novi: African Journalism Studies* 33, no. 1 (2012): 54–65. https://doi.org/10.1080/02560054.2011.636828.

Giddens, Anthony. *The Constitution of Society: Outline of the Theory of Structuration*. Berkeley: University of California Press, 1984.

Gilbert, Jeremy. "AI Finally Becomes Helpful." *Nieman Lab* (blog), January 2019. https://www.niemanlab.org/2019/01/ai-finally-becomes-helpful.

Glaser, Barney G., and Anselm L. Strauss. *The Discovery of Grounded Theory: Strategies for Qualitative Research*. New York: Aldine de Gruyter, 1967.

Goldman Sachs Group. *Virtual and Augmented Reality: Understanding the Race for the Next Computing Platform*. New York: Goldman Sachs Global Investment Research, 2016. https://www.goldmansachs.com/insights/pages/technology-driving-innovation-folder/virtual-and-augmented-reality/report.pdf.

Goodman, Russell. "Transcendentalism." In *The Stanford Encyclopedia of Philosophy*, edited by Edward N. Zalta. Metaphysics Research Lab, Stanford University, 2019. https://plato.stanford.edu/entries/transcendentalism/.

Greenfield, Rebecca. "What the New York Times's 'Snow Fall' Means to Online Journalism's Future." *The Atlantic*, December 20, 2012. https://www.theatlantic.com/technology/archive/2012/12/new-york-times-snow-fall-feature/320253.

Griffith, Erin. "Why Startups Fail, According to Their Founders." *Fortune*, September 25, 2014. https://fortune.com/2014/09/25/why-startups-fail-according-to-their-founders.

Grossman, Lawrence K. *The Electronic Republic: Reshaping Democracy in the Information Age*. New York: Viking, 1995.

Gunaratne, Shelton A. "Buddhist Goals of Journalism and the News Paradigm." *Javnost—The Public* 16, no. 2 (2009): 61–75. https://doi.org/10.1080/13183222.2009.11009004.

———. "Paper, Printing and the Printing Press: A Horizontally Integrative Macrohistory Analysis." *Gazette* 63, no. 6 (2001): 459–79. https://doi.org/10.1177/0016549201063006001.

Gunaratne, Shelton A., Mark Pearson, and Sugath Senarath. *Mindful Journalism and News Ethics in the Digital Era: A Buddhist Approach*. New York: Routledge, 2015.

Haim, Mario, Andreas Graefe, and Hans-Bernd Brosius. "Burst of the Filter Bubble? Effects of Personalization on the Diversity of Google News." *Digital Journalism* 6, no. 3 (2018): 330–43. https://doi.org/10.1080/21670811.2017.1338145.

Hamby, Chris. "Inside the Global 'Club' That Helps Executives Escape Their Crimes." *BuzzFeed News*, August 28, 2016. https://www.buzzfeednews.com/article/chrishamby/super-court.

Hamilton, James T. *Democracy's Detectives: The Economics of Investigative Journalism*. Cambridge, MA: Harvard University Press, 2016.

Hampton, Mark. *Visions of the Press in Britain, 1850–1950*. Urbana: University of Illinois Press, 2004.

Hanh, Thich Nhat. *The Miracle of Mindfulness: An Introduction to the Practice of Meditation*. Translated by Mobi Ho. Boston: Beacon Press, 1975.

Hanqi, Fang. *A History of Journalism in China: Volume 1*. Singapore: Silkroad Press, 2013.

Hartman, John. "USA Today Is Turning 30, in Danger of 'Marking 30.'" *Editor and Publisher*, September 12, 2012. https://

web.archive.org/web/20161025050132
/http://www.editorandpublisher.com
/columns/usa-today-is-turning-30-in
-danger-of-marking-30/.

Hassan, Robert. "Digitality, Virtual Reality and the 'Empathy Machine.'" *Digital Journalism* 8, no. 2 (2020): 195–212. https://doi.org/10.1080/21670811.2018 .1517604.

Herian, Robert. "The Politics of Blockchain." *Law and Critique* 29, no. 2 (2018): 129–31. https://doi.org/10.1007/s10978 -018-9223-1.

Hermida, Alfred. *Tell Everyone: Why We Share and Why It Matters.* Toronto: Double-day Canada, 2014.

Hermida, Alfred, Seth C. Lewis, and Rodrigo Zamith. "Sourcing the Arab Spring: A Case Study of Andy Carvin's Sources on Twitter During the Tunisian and Egyptian Revolutions." *Journal of Computer-Mediated Communication* 19, no. 3 (2014): 479–99. https://doi.org /10.1111/jcc4.12074.

Herrera, Fernanda, Jeremy Bailenson, Erika Weisz, Elise Ogle, and Jamil Zaki. "Building Long-Term Empathy: A Large-Scale Comparison of Traditional and Virtual Reality Perspective-Taking." *PLOS ONE* 13, no. 10 (2018): e0204494. https://doi.org/10 .1371/journal.pone.0204494.

Holmes, Aaron. "From Snap to Uber, Here Are 9 Billion-Dollar Tech Companies That Still Aren't Profitable." *Business Insider*, November 27, 2019. https:// www.businessinsider.com/tech -companies-worth-billions-unprof itable-tesla-uber-snap-2019-11.

Huang, Edgar, Karen Davison, Stephanie Shreve, Twila Davis, Elizabeth Bet-tendorf, and Anita Nair. "Facing the Challenges of Convergence: Media Professionals' Concerns of Working Across Media Platforms." *Convergence* 12, no. 1 (2006): 83–98. https:// doi.org/10.1177/1354856506061557.

Ingram, Matthew. "A Civil Primer: The Benefits, and Pitfalls, of a New Media Ecosystem." *Columbia Journalism Review*, August 13, 2018. https://www.cjr.org/ business_of_news/civil.php.

Israel, Mae. "On the Table: Reinventing Civic Dialogue." *Knight Foundation* (blog). February 26, 2018. https://knight foundation.org/articles/on-the-table -reinventing-civic-dialogue.

Ivancsics, Bernat. *Blockchain in Journalism.* New York: Tow Center for Digital Journalism, 2019. https://www.cjr.org /tow_center_reports/blockchain-in -journalism.php.

Jones, Matthew R., and Helena Karsten. "Giddens's Structuration Theory and Information Systems Research." *MIS Quarterly* 32, no. 1 (2008): 127–57. https://doi.org/10.2307/25148831.

Josephi, Beate. "How Much Democracy Does Journalism Need?" *Journalism* 14, no. 4 (2013): 474–89. https://doi.org/10 .1177/1464884912464172.

Kabat-Zinn, Jon. "Mindfulness-Based Interventions in Context: Past, Present, and Future." *Clinical Psychology: Science and Practice* 10, no. 2 (2003): 144–56. https://doi.org/10.1093/clipsy .bpg016.

Kamenetz, Anya. "How Upworthy Used Emotional Data to Become the Fastest Growing Media Site of All Time." *Fast Company*, June 7, 2013. https:// www.fastcompany.com/3012649/how -upworthy-used-emotional-data-to -become-the-fastest-growing-media -site-of-all-time.

Kane, Gerald C., Anh Nguyen Phillips, Jonathan R. Copulsky, and Garth R. Andrus. *The Technology Fallacy: How People Are the Real Key to Digital Transformation.* Cambridge, MA: MIT Press, 2019.

Kang, Jay Caspian. "Should Reddit Be Blamed for the Spreading of a Smear?" *New York Times*, July 25, 2013. https://www .nytimes.com/2013/07/28/magazine /should-reddit-be-blamed-for-the -spreading-of-a-smear.html.

Kang, Seok, Erin O'Brien, Arturo Villarreal, Wansoo Lee, and Chad Mahood. "Immersive Journalism and Telepresence." *Digital Journalism* 7, no. 2 (2019): 294–313. https://doi.org/10 .1080/21670811.2018.1504624.

Kanter, Rosabeth Moss, Barry Stein, and Todd Jick, eds. *The Challenge of Organizational Change: How Companies Experience It and Leaders Guide It.* New York: Free Press, 1992.

Kasireddy, Preethi. "Why TruStory Is Shutting Down." *Medium* (blog), January 30, 2020. https://medium.com/trustory-app/why-trustory-is-shutting-down-6d50175628eb.

Kenneally, Christine. "We Saw Nuns Kill Children: The Ghosts of St. Joseph's Catholic Orphanage." *BuzzFeed News*, August 27, 2018. https://www.buzzfeednews.com/article/christinekenneally/orphanage-death-catholic-abuse-nuns-st-josephs.

Kent, Tom. "An Ethical Reality Check for Virtual Reality Journalism." *Medium* (blog), February 28, 2016. https://medium.com/@tjrkent/an-ethical-reality-check-for-virtual-reality-journalism-8e5230673507.

Khondker, Habibul Haque. "Role of the New Media in the Arab Spring." *Globalizations* 8, no. 5 (2011): 675–79. https://doi.org/10.1080/14747731.2011.621287.

Kim, Violet. "Virtual Reality, Real Grief." *Slate*, May 27, 2020. https://slate.com/technology/2020/05/meeting-you-virtual-reality-documentary-mbc.html.

Kirschenbaum, Matthew G. *Track Changes: A Literary History of Word Processing*. Cambridge, MA: Harvard University Press, 2016.

Kline, Ronald R. *Consumers in the Country: Technology and Social Change in Rural America*. Baltimore: Johns Hopkins University Press, 2000.

———. "Technological Determinism." In *International Encyclopedia of the Social and Behavioral Sciences*, edited by N. J. Smelser and B. Baltes, 15495–98. Oxford: Pergamon Press, 2001.

Kovach, Bill, and Tom Rosenstiel. *The Elements of Journalism: What Newspeople Should Know and the Public Should Expect*. New York: Crown, 2001.

Krugman, Paul. "Why Most Economists' Predictions Are Wrong." *Red Herring* 55 (June 1998). http://web.archive.org/web/19980610100009/www.redherring.com/mag/issue55/economics.html#?hn.

Küng, Lucy. *Going Digital: A Roadmap for Organisational Transformation*. Oxford: Reuters Institute for the Study of Journalism, 2017.

———. *Innovators in Digital News*. London: I.B. Tauris, 2015.

Lajqi, Margarita, and Juliane A. Lischka. "Normative Principles in Newsroom Innovation. The Case of 360° Video Adoption by Editorial Knowledge Champions." *Journal of Media Innovations* 7, no. 1 (2021). https://doi.org/10.5617/jomi.6524.

Larson, Magali S. *The Rise of Professionalism: A Sociological Analysis*. Berkeley: University of California Press, 1977.

Lasorsa, Dominic L., Seth C. Lewis, and Avery E. Holton. "Normalizing Twitter." *Journalism Studies* 13, no. 1 (2012): 19–36. https://doi.org/10.1080/1461670X.2011.571825.

Laufer, Peter. *Slow News: A Manifesto for the Critical News Consumer*. Salem: Oregon State University Press, 2014.

Lawrence, Regina G., Eric Gordon, Andrew DeVigal, C. Mellor, and J. Elbaz. *Building Engagement: Supporting the Practice of Relational Journalism*. Portland, OR: Agora Journalism Center, 2019. https://agora.uoregon.edu/2019/04/01/building-engagement-a-report-on-supporting-the-practice-of-relational-journalism/.

Lawrence, Regina G., Damian Radcliffe, and Thomas R. Schmidt. "Practicing Engagement: Participatory Journalism in the Web 2.0 Era." *Journalism Practice* 12, no. 10 (2018): 1220–40. https://doi.org/10.1080/17512786.2017.1391712.

Laws, Ana Luisa Sánchez. "Can Immersive Journalism Enhance Empathy?" *Digital Journalism* 8, no. 2 (2020): 213–28. https://doi.org/10.1080/21670811.2017.1389286.

Lehtisaari, Katja, Mikko Villi, Mikko Grönlund, Carl-Gustav Lindén, Bozena I. Mierzejewska, Robert Picard, and Axel Roepnack. "Comparing Innovation and Social Media Strategies in Scandinavian and US Newspapers." *Digital Journalism* 6, no. 8 (2018): 1029–40. https://doi.org/10.1080/21670811.2018.1503061.

Le Masurier, Megan. "What Is Slow Journalism?" *Journalism Practice* 9, no. 2

(2015): 138–52. https://doi.org/10.1080/17512786.2014.916471.

"Letter from the Staff: A New Year's Wish from B&C." *Broadcasting and Cable,* January 3, 2011. https://www.broadcastingcable.com/news/letter-staff-new-years-wish-bc-111509.

"Letter from the Staff: OK, We Can Do This." *Broadcasting and Cable,* January 2, 2012. https://www.broadcastingcable.com/news/letter-staff-ok-we-cando-112738.

Lewis, Seth C. "From Journalism to Information: The Transformation of the Knight Foundation and News Innovation." *Mass Communication and Society* 15, no. 3 (2012): 309–34. https://doi.org/10.1080/15205436.2011.611607.

———. "The Tension Between Professional Control and Open Participation." *Information, Communication and Society* 15, no. 6 (2012): 836–66. https://doi.org/10.1080/1369118X.2012.674150.

Lewis, Seth C., and Logan Molyneux. "A Decade of Research on Social Media and Journalism: Assumptions, Blind Spots, and a Way Forward." *Media and Communication* 6, no. 4 (2018): 11–23. https://doi.org/10.17645/mac.v6i4.1562.

Lichterman, Joseph. "How Germany's Die Zeit Is Trying to Reach a Younger Audience (While Also Putting up a Paywall)." *Nieman Lab* (blog), May 10, 2017. https://www.niemanlab.org/2017/05/how-germanys-die-zeit-is-trying-to-reach-a-younger-audience-while-also-putting-up-a-paywall.

Liu, Chang-de. "De-skilling Effects on Journalists: ICTs and the Labour Process of Taiwanese Newspaper Reporters." *Canadian Journal of Communication* 31, no. 3 (2006): 695–714. https://doi.org/10.22230/cjc.2006v31n3a1763.

Locke, Wilson. "Telecommunication in the News Industry: The Newsroom Before and After Computers." In *People and Technology in the Workplace,* edited by National Academy of Engineering and National Research Council, 279–95. Washington, DC: National Academic Press, 1991.

Lowrey, Wilson. "Normative Conflict in the Newsroom: The Case of Digital Photo Manipulation." *Journal of Mass Media Ethics* 18, no. 2 (2003): 123–42. https://doi.org/10.1207/S15327728JMME1802_05.

———. "Routine News: The Power of the Organization in Visual Journalism." *Visual Communication Quarterly* 6, no. 2 (1999): 10–15. https://doi.org/10.1080/15551399909363404.

Luo, Tian, and Amar Mann. "Survival and Growth of Silicon Valley High-Tech Businesses Born in 2000." *Monthly Labor Review,* September 2011, 16–31.

MacKenzie, Donald A., and Judy Wajcman. *The Social Shaping of Technology.* London: Open University Press, 1999.

Madary, Michael, and Thomas K. Metzinger. "Real Virtuality: A Code of Ethical Conduct. Recommendations for Good Scientific Practice and the Consumers of VR-Technology." *Frontiers in Robotics and AI* 3 (2016). https://doi.org/10.3389/frobt.2016.00003.

Man, John. *The Gutenberg Revolution.* New York: Random House, 2010.

Manjoo, Farhad. "A Whole Lot of Bells, Way Too Many Whistles." *Slate,* August 15, 2013. http://www.slate.com/articles/technology/technology/2013/08/snow_fall_the_jockey_the_scourge_of_the_new_york_times_bell_and_whistle.html.

Marchi, Anna. *Self-Reflexive Journalism: A Corpus Study of Journalistic Culture and Community in "The Guardian."* London: Routledge, 2019.

Marcus, Gary, and Ernest Davis. *Rebooting AI: Building Artificial Intelligence We Can Trust.* New York: Knopf Doubleday, 2019.

Margolis, Michael, and David Resnick. *Politics as Usual: The Cyberspace "Revolution."* Thousand Oaks, CA: Sage, 2000.

Mari, Will. *A Short History of Disruptive Journalism Technologies: 1960–1990.* London: Routledge, 2019.

Marjoribanks, Timothy. "The 'Anti-Wapping'? Technological Innovation and Workplace Reorganization at the Financial Times." *Media, Culture and Society* 22, no. 5 (2000): 575–93. https://doi.org/10.1177/016344300022005003.

Markides, Constantinos. "Disruptive Innovation: In Need of Better Theory."

129

Journal of Product Innovation Management 23, no. 1 (2006): 19–25. https://doi.org/10.1111/j.1540-5885.2005.00177.x.

Martin, C. Dianne. "The Myth of the Awesome Thinking Machine." *Communications of the ACM* 36, no. 4 (1993): 120–33. https://doi.org/10.1145/255950.153587.

McChesney, Robert W. *Rich Media, Poor Democracy: Communication Politics in Dubious Times.* New York: New Press, 2015.

McChesney, Robert W., and John Nichols. *The Death and Life of American Journalism: The Media Revolution That Will Begin the World Again.* New York: Public Affairs, 2010.

McIntyre, Karen, and Cathrine Gyldensted. "Constructive Journalism: An Introduction and Practical Guide for Applying Positive Psychology Techniques to News Production." *Journal of Media Innovations* 4, no. 2 (2018): 20–34. https://doi.org/10.5617/jomi.v4i2.2403.

McLuhan, Marshall. *The Gutenberg Galaxy: The Making of Typographic Man.* Toronto: University of Toronto Press, 1962.

McMurtrie, Douglas C. *The Book: The Story of Printing and Bookmaking.* New York: Hippocrene, 1990.

McNair, Brian. *The Sociology of Journalism.* London: Bloomsbury Academic, 1998.

Meyer, Philip. *The Vanishing Newspaper: Saving Journalism in the Information Age.* Columbia: University of Missouri Press, 2009.

Milk, Chris. "How Virtual Reality Can Create the Ultimate Empathy Machine." Filmed March 2015 in Vancouver. TED video, 10:16. https://www.ted.com/talks/chris_milk_how_virtual_reality_can_create_the_ultimate_empathy_machine.

Min, Seong Jae. *As Democracy Goes, So Does Journalism: Evolution of Journalism in Liberal, Deliberative, and Participatory Democracy.* Lanham, MD: Lexington Books, 2018.

———. "Conversation Through Journalism: Searching for Organizing Principles of Public and Citizen Journalism."

Journalism 17, no. 5 (2016): 567–82. https://doi.org/10.1177/1464884915571298.

———. "Occupy Wall Street and Deliberative Decision-Making: Translating Theory to Practice." *Communication, Culture and Critique* 8, no. 1 (2015): 73–89. https://doi.org/10.1111/cccr.12074.

———. "What the Twenty-First-Century Engaged Journalism Can Learn from the Twentieth-Century Public Journalism." *Journalism Practice* 14, no. 5 (2020): 626–41. https://doi.org/10.1080/17512786.2020.1758188.

Min, Seong Jae, and Donghee Yvette Wohn. "All the News That You Don't like: Cross-Cutting Exposure and Political Participation in the Age of Social Media." *Computers in Human Behavior* 83 (2018): 24–31. https://doi.org/10.1016/j.chb.2018.01.015.

———. "Underneath the Filter Bubble: The Role of Weak Ties and Network Cultural Diversity in Cross-Cutting Exposure to Disagreements on Social Media." *Journal of Social Media in Society* 9, no. 1 (2020): 22–38. https://thejsms.org/index.php/TSMRI/article/view/447.

Mindich, David T. Z. *Just the Facts: How "Objectivity" Came to Define American Journalism.* New York: NYU Press, 2000.

Misa, Thomas J. "How Machines Make History, and How Historians (And Others) Help Them to Do So." *Science, Technology, and Human Values* 13, nos. 3–4 (1988): 308–31. https://doi.org/10.1177/016224398801303-410.

Moglen, Eben. "Considering Zenger: Partisan Politics and the Legal Profession in Provincial New York." *Columbia Law Review* 94 (1994): 1495–1524.

Molyneux, Logan, Seth C. Lewis, and Avery E. Holton. "Media Work, Identity, and the Motivations That Shape Branding Practices Among Journalists: An Explanatory Framework." *New Media and Society* 21, no. 4 (2019): 836–55. https://doi.org/10.1177/1461444818809392.

Moody, Robert E., and Richard C. Simmons. *The Glorious Revolution in Massachusetts: Selected Documents, 1689–1692.*

Boston: Colonial Society of Massachusetts, 1988.

Mukherjee, Siddhartha. "How Does the Coronavirus Behave Inside a Patient?" *New Yorker*, April 6, 2020. https://www.newyorker.com/magazine/2020/04/06/how-does-the-coronavirus-behave-inside-a-patient.

Mutter, Alan. "Big Data Is a Big Deal for Newspapers." *Editor and Publisher* 145, no. 8 (August 2012): 20–21.

Natale, Simone, and Andrea Ballatore. "Imagining the Thinking Machine: Technological Myths and the Rise of Artificial Intelligence." *Convergence* 26, no. 1 (2020): 3–18. https://doi.org/10.1177/1354856517715164.

Negroponte, Nicholas. *Being Digital*. New York: Vintage, 1995.

Nelson, Jacob L. "And Deliver Us to Segmentation: The Growing Appeal of the Niche News Audience." *Journalism Practice* 12, no. 2 (2018): 204–19. https://doi.org/10.1080/17512786.2017.1378588.

Newquist, Harvey. *The Brain Makers: Genius, Ego, and Greed in the Quest for Machines That Think*. Indianapolis: Sams, 1984.

"Newspapers Fact Sheet." *Pew Research Center*, July 9, 2019. https://www.journalism.org/fact-sheet/newspapers.

Nietzsche, Friedrich. *The Dawn of Day*. Translated by John M. Kennedy. New York: Macmillan Company, 1911.

Nip, Joyce. "The Last Days of Civic Journalism: The Case of the Savannah Morning News." Journalism Practice 2, no. 2 (2008): 179-96. https://doi.org/10.1080/17512780801999352.

Noble, Safiya Umoja. *Algorithms of Oppression: How Search Engines Reinforce Racism*. New York: NYU Press, 2018.

O'Neil, Cathy. *Weapons of Math Destruction: How Big Data Increases Inequality and Threatens Democracy*. New York: Crown/Archetype, 2016.

Orlikowski, Wanda J. "The Duality of Technology: Rethinking the Concept of Technology in Organizations." *Organization Science* 3, no. 3 (1992): 398–427.

———. "Using Technology and Constituting Structures: A Practice Lens for Studying Technology in Organizations."

Organization Science 11, no. 4 (2000): 404–28. https://doi.org/10.1287/orsc.11.4.404.14600.

Örnebring, Henrik. "Technology and Journalism-as-Labour: Historical Perspectives." *Journalism* 11, no. 1 (2010): 57–74. https://doi.org/10.1177/1464884909350644.

Örnebring, Henrik, and Claudia Mellado. "Valued Skills Among Journalists: An Exploratory Comparison of Six European Nations." *Journalism* 19, no. 4 (2018): 445–63. https://doi.org/10.1177/1464884916657514.

Parkins, Wendy, and Geoffrey Craig. *Slow Living*. Oxford: Berg, 2006.

Pasquale, Frank. *The Black Box Society*. Cambridge, MA: Harvard University Press, 2015.

Pavlik, John. "The Impact of Technology on Journalism." *Journalism Studies* 1, no. 2 (2000): 229–37. https://doi.org/10.1080/14616700050028226.

———. "Innovation and the Future of Journalism." *Digital Journalism* 1, no. 2 (2013): 181–93. https://doi.org/10.1080/21670811.2012.756666.

———. *Journalism and New Media*. New York: Columbia University Press, 2001.

Pearson, Mark, Cait McMahon, and Analise O'Donovan. "Potential Benefits of Teaching Mindfulness to Journalism Students." *Asia Pacific Media Educator* 28, no. 2 (2018): 186–204. https://doi.org/10.1177/1326365X18800080.

Perrow, Charles. *Complex Organizations: A Critical Essay*. New York: Random House, 1986.

Peters, Jeremy W. "Web Focus Helps Revitalize The Atlantic." *New York Times*, December 12, 2010. https://www.nytimes.com/2010/12/13/business/media/13atlantic.html.

Peterson, Becky. "At The New Yorker Festival, Non-Subscribers Outnumber Brand Devotees." *Folio*, October 17, 2016. https://www.foliomag.com/new-yorker-festival-non-subscribers-outnumber-brand-devotees.

Petre, Caitlin. "Engineering Consent." *Digital Journalism* 6, no. 4 (2018): 509–27. https://doi.org/10.1080/21670811.2018.1444998.

Pettegree, Andrew. *The Invention of News: How the World Came to Know About Itself*. New Haven, CT: Yale University Press, 2014.

Picard, Robert G. "Changing Business Models of Online Content Services: Their Implications for Multimedia and Other Content Producers." *International Journal on Media Management* 2, no. 2 (2000): 60–68. https://doi.org /10.1080/14241270009389923.

Pinch, Trevor J., and Wiebe E. Bijker. "The Social Construction of Facts and Artefacts: Or How the Sociology of Science and the Sociology of Technology Might Benefit Each Other." *Social Studies of Science* 14, no. 3 (1984): 399–441.

Porcu, Ornella. "Exploring Innovative Learning Culture in the Newsroom." *Journalism* 21, no. 10 (2017): 1556–72. https://doi.org/10.1177/14648849177 24596.

Porter, Michael E. *Competitive Advantage: Creating and Sustaining Superior Performance*. New York: Free Press, 1998.

Porwancher, Andrew. "Objectivity's Prophet: Adolph S. Ochs and the *New York Times*, 1896–1935." *Journalism History* 36, no. 4 (2011): 186–95. https://doi .org/10.1080/00947679.2011.12062831.

Posetti, Julie. *Time to Step Away from the "Bright, Shiny Things"? Towards a Sustainable Model of Journalism Innovation in an Era of Perpetual Change*. Oxford: Reuters Institute for the Study of Journalism, 2018.

Posetti, Julie, Felix Simon, and Nabeelah Shabbir. *What If Scale Breaks Community? Rebooting Audience Engagement When Journalism Is Under Fire*. Oxford: Reuters Institute for the Study of Journalism, 2019.

Pöttker, Horst. "News and Its Communicative Quality: The Inverted Pyramid— When and Why Did It Appear?" *Journalism Studies* 4, no. 4 (2003): 501–11. https://doi.org/10.1080 /1461670032000136596.

Powers, Matthew. "'In Forms That Are Familiar and Yet-to-Be Invented': American Journalism and the Discourse of Technologically Specific Work." *Journal of Communication Inquiry* 36, no. 1 (2012): 24–43. https:// doi.org/10.1177/0196859911426009.

———. "The New Boots on the Ground: NGOs in the Changing Landscape of International News." *Journalism* 17, no. 4 (2016): 401–16. https://doi.org /10.1177/1464884914568077.

Przyblyski, Jeannene M. "Revolution at a Standstill: Photography and the Paris Commune of 1871." *Yale French Studies*, no. 101 (2001): 54–78. https:// doi.org/10.2307/3090606.

"Public Trust in Government Remains Near Historic Lows as Partisan Attitudes Shift." *Pew Research Center*, May 3, 2017. http://www.people-press.org /2017/05/03/public-trust-in-govern ment-remains-near-historic-lows-as -partisan-attitudes-shift.

Quinn, Stephen. *Conversations on Convergence: Insiders' Views on News Production in the 21st Century*. New York: Peter Lang, 2006.

Ralon, Laureano. "Beyond Categorization: Marshall McLuhan, Technological Determinism, and Social Science Methodology—a Reappraisal." MA thesis, Simon Fraser University, 2009. https://summit.sfu.ca/item/9348.

Rashidian, Nushin, Peter D. Brown, Elizabeth Hansen, Emily J. Bell, and Jonathan R. Albright. *Friend and Foe: The Platform Press at the Heart of Journalism*. New York: Tow Center for Digital Journalism, 2018. https://doi.org /10.7916/d8-15pq-x415.

Rauch, Jennifer. *Slow Media: Why Slow Is Satisfying, Sustainable, and Smart*. New York: Oxford University Press, 2018.

Rheingold, Howard. *The Virtual Community: Homesteading on the Electronic Frontier*. Boston: Addison-Wesley, 1993.

Ridley, Matt. "Don't Write Off the Next Big Thing Too Soon." *Times*, November 6, 2017. https://www.thetimes.co.uk /article/dont-write-off-the-next-big -thing-too-soon-rbf2q9sck.

Roberts, Graham, and Jonathan Corum. "How We Augmented Our Original Reporting of the Moon Landing for Its 50th Anniversary." *New York Times*, July 19, 2019. https://www

.nytimes.com/2019/07/19/reader-center/apollo-11-moon-landing-augmented-reality.html.

Rogers, Everett M. *Communication Technology*. New York: Simon and Schuster, 1986.

———. *Diffusion of Innovations*. New York: Free Press, 1995.

Rosen, Deborah A. "The Supreme Court of Judicature of Colonial New York: Civil Practice in Transition, 1691–1760." *Law and History Review* 5, no. 1 (1987): 213–47. https://doi.org/10.2307/743941.

Rosen, Jay. *What Are Journalists For?* New Haven, CT: Yale University Press, 1999.

Rosenberg, Howard, and Charles S. Feldman. *No Time to Think: The Menace of Media Speed and the 24-Hour News Cycle*. New York: Continuum, 2008.

Royal, Cindy. "Are Journalism Schools Teaching Their Students the Right Skills?" *Nieman Lab* (blog), April 28, 2014. https://www.niemanlab.org/2014/04/cindy-royal-are-journalism-schools-teaching-their-students-the-right-skills.

Russial, John T. "Pagination and the Newsroom: A Question of Time." *Newspaper Research Journal* 15, no. 1 (1994): 91–101. https://doi.org/10.1177/073953299401500110.

Ryckman, Larry. "Colorado Sun Wins 28 Awards, Including 14 First-Place, in Top of the Rockies Competition." *Colorado Sun*, April 20, 2020. https://coloradosun.com/2020/04/20/colorado-sun-top-of-the-rockies-spj-awards.

———. "From the Editor: Civil Is Gone, but The Colorado Sun Is Still Rising." *Colorado Sun*, June 4, 2020. https://coloradosun.com/2020/06/04/colorado-sun-media-journalism-newspapers-opinion.

Ryfe, David M. *Can Journalism Survive? An Inside Look at American Newsrooms*. Malden, MA: Polity, 2012.

———. *Journalism and the Public*. Malden, MA: Polity, 2017.

Saba, Jennifer. "Beyond Cute Cats: How BuzzFeed Is Reinventing Itself." *Reuters*, February 23, 2014. https://www.reuters.com/article/us-usa-media-buzzfeed-idUSBREA1M0IQ20140223.

Sanders, Sam. "Upworthy Was One of the Hottest Sites Ever: You Won't Believe What Happened Next." *NPR*, June 20, 2017. https://www.npr.org/sections/alltechconsidered/2017/06/20/533529538/upworthy-was-one-of-the-hottest-sites-ever-you-wont-believe-what-happened-next.

Scanlan, Christopher Chip. "Birth of the Inverted Pyramid: A Child of Technology, Commerce and History." *Poynter*, June 20, 2003. https://www.poynter.org/reporting-editing/2003/birth-of-the-inverted-pyramid-a-child-of-technology-commerce-and-history.

Schantin, Dietmar. "Innovation Matters." *Editor and Publisher* 151, no. 7 (2018): 33–37.

Schreiber, Martin, and Clemens Zimmermann, eds. *Journalism and Technological Change: Historical Perspectives, Contemporary Trends*. Frankfurt: Campus Verlag, 2014.

Schudson, Michael. "The Objectivity Norm in American Journalism." *Journalism* 2, no. 2 (2001): 149–70. https://doi.org/10.1177/146488490100200201.

———. *Why Journalism Still Matters*. Hoboken, NJ: Wiley, 2018.

Schudson, Michael, and Chris Anderson. "Objectivity, Professionalism, and Truth Seeking in Journalism." In *The Handbook of Journalism Studies*, edited by Karin Wahl-Jorgensen and Thomas Hanitzsch, 88–101. London: Routledge, 2008.

Senarath, Sugath. "The Journalist and the Middle Path." In *Mindful Journalism and News Ethics in the Digital Era: A Buddhist Approach*, edited by Shelton A. Gunaratne, Mark Pearson, and Sugath Senarath, 130–42. New York: Routledge, 2015.

Shilina, Sasha. "Journalism + Blockchain: Possible Solution for an Industry Crisis?" *Medium* (blog), September 11, 2019. https://medium.com/paradigm-fund/journalism-blockchain-possible-solution-for-an-industry-crisis-becd6da3714f.

Siebert, Fred Seaton, Theodore Peterson, and Wilbur Schramm. *Four Theories of the Press: The Authoritarian, Libertarian, Social Responsibility, and Soviet Communist Concepts of What the Press Should Be and Do*. Urbana: University of Illinois Press, 1956.

Singer, Jane B. "The Political J-Blogger: 'Normalizing' a New Media Form to Fit Old Norms and Practices." *Journalism* 6, no. 2 (2005): 173–98. https://doi.org/10.1177/1464884905051009.

Sloan, David. "Chaos, Polemics, and America's First Newspaper." *Journalism Quarterly* 70, no. 3 (1993): 666–81. https://doi.org/10.1177/107769909307000317.

"The Smart, the Stupid, and the Catastrophically Scary: An Interview with an Anonymous Data Scientist." *Logic*, no. 1 (2017). https://logicmag.io/intelligence/interview-with-an-anonymous-data-scientist.

Smith, Merritt Roe, and Leo Marx. *Does Technology Drive History? The Dilemma of Technological Determinism*. Cambridge, MA: MIT Press, 1994.

Smolkin, Rachel. "Adapt or Die." *American Journalism Review* 28, no. 3 (July 2006): 16–23. https://ajrarchive.org/Article.asp?id=4111.

Spinks, David. "Distributed Control: How Reddit Is Taking the Management Out of Community Management." *CMX* (blog), June 9, 2014. https://cmxhub.com/erik-martin-reddit-community-interview.

Spyridou, Lia-Paschalia, Maria Matsiola, Andreas Veglis, George Kalliris, and Charalambos Dimoulas. "Journalism in a State of Flux: Journalists as Agents of Technology Innovation and Emerging News Practices." *International Communication Gazette* 75, no. 1 (2013): 76–98. https://doi.org/10.1177/1748048512461763.

Steensen, Steen. "What's Stopping Them?" *Journalism Studies* 10, no. 6 (2009): 821–36. https://doi.org/10.1080/14616700902975087.

Stensaas, Harlan S. "The Objective News Report: A Content Analysis of Selected U.S. Daily Newspapers for 1865 to 1954 (Ethics, Professionalism, United States)." PhD diss., University of Southern Mississippi, 1987. https://aquila.usm.edu/theses_dissertations/2946.

Stephens, Mitchell. *A History of News*. 3rd ed. New York: Oxford University Press, 2006.

Stepp, Carl Sessions. "Maybe It Is Time to Panic." *American Journalism Review* 30, no. 2 (May 2008): 22–27. https://ajrarchive.org/article.asp?id=4491.

Stevens, Harry. "Why Outbreaks Like Coronavirus Spread Exponentially, and How to 'Flatten the Curve.'" *Washington Post*, March 14, 2020. https://www.washingtonpost.com/graphics/2020/world/corona-simulator/.

Stray, Jonathan. "The Age of the Cyborg." *Columbia Journalism Review*, Fall/Winter 2016. https://www.cjr.org/analysis/cyborg_virtual_reality_reuters_tracer.php.

Stringer, Paul. "Finding a Place in the Journalistic Field: The Pursuit of Recognition and Legitimacy at BuzzFeed and Vice." *Journalism Studies* 19, no. 13 (2018): 1991–2000. https://doi.org/10.1080/1461670X.2018.1496027.

Stroh, Sean. "An Artificial World." *Editor and Publisher* 150, no. 12 (December 2017): 33–37.

Suciu, Peter. "A New Perception." *Editor and Publisher* 151, no. 4 (April 2018): 36–43.

Swartz, Lana. "Blockchain Dreams: Imagining Techno-Economic Alternatives After Bitcoin." In *Another Economy Is Possible: Culture and Economy in a Time of Crisis*, edited by Manuel Castells, 82–105. Malden, MA: Polity, 2017.

Sylvie, George, and Patricia D. Witherspoon. *Time, Change, and the American Newspaper*. Mahwah, NJ: Lawrence Erlbaum Associates, 2001.

Taddonio, Patrice. "After Solitary." *Frontline*, April 18, 2017. https://www.pbs.org/wgbh/frontline/article/after-solitary.

Tandoc, Edson. "Five Ways BuzzFeed Is Preserving (or Transforming) the Journalistic Field." *Journalism* 19, no. 2 (2018): 200–216. https://doi.org/10.1177/1464884917691785.

———. "Journalism Is Twerking? How Web Analytics Is Changing the Process of Gatekeeping." *New Media and Society*

16, no. 4 (2014): 559–75. https://doi
.org/10.1177/1461444814530541.

Tandoc, Edson, and Julian Maitra. "News
Organizations' Use of Native Videos
on Facebook: Tweaking the Journalistic Field One Algorithm Change at
a Time." *New Media and Society* 20,
no. 5 (2018): 1679–96. https://doi.org
/10.1177/1461444817702398.

Tarr, Joel A., Thomas Finholt, and David
Goodman. "The City and the Telegraph: Urban Telecommunications in
the Pre-Telephone Era." *Journal of
Urban History* 14, no. 1 (1987): 38–80.
https://doi.org/10.1177/0096144287
01400103.

Tong, Jingrong, and Landong Zuo. "The
Inapplicability of Objectivity:
Understanding the Work of Data
Journalism." *Journalism Practice* 15,
no. 2 (2021): 153–69. https://doi.org
/10.1080/17512786.2019.1698974.

"The Trust Machine." *Economist*, October
31, 2015. https://www.economist
.com/leaders/2015/10/31/the-trust
-machine.

Tsien, Tsuen-Hsuin. *Science and Civilisation
in China*. Vol. 5, *Chemistry and Chemi-
cal Technology*. Part 1, *Paper and Printing*. Edited by Joseph Needham.
Cambridge: Cambridge University
Press, 1985

US Senate. *The Future of Journalism: Hearing
Before the Subcommittee on Communications, Technology, and the Internet of
the Committee on Commerce, Science,
and Transportation* (Washington, DC:
US Government Printing Office,
2010). https://www.govinfo.gov
/content/pkg/CHRG-111shrg52162
/pdf/CHRG-111shrg52162.pdf.

Usher, Nikki. *Interactive Journalism: Hackers,
Data, and Code*. Urbana: University of
Illinois Press, 2016.

———. *Making News at the "New York Times."*
Ann Arbor: University of Michigan
Press, 2014.

Vázquez Sampere, Juan Pablo, Martin J.
Bienenstock, and Ezra W. Zuckerman. "Debating Disruptive Innovation." *MIT Sloan Management Review*,
Spring 2016. https://sloanreview.mit
.edu/article/debating-disruptive
-innovation.

Vos, Tim P., and Stephanie Craft. "The Discursive Construction of Journalistic
Transparency." *Journalism Studies* 18,
no. 12 (2017): 1505–22. https://doi.org
/10.1080/1461670X.2015.1135754.

Vos, Tim P., and Gregory P. Perreault.
"The Discursive Construction of
the Gamification of Journalism."
Convergence 26, no. 3 (2020): 470–85.
https://doi.org/10.1177/1354856520
909542.

Vos, Tim P., and Jane B. Singer. "Media Discourse About Entrepreneurial Journalism." *Journalism Practice* 10, no. 2
(2016): 143–59. https://doi.org/10
.1080/17512786.2015.1124730.

Waisbord, Silvio. *Reinventing Professionalism:
Journalism and News in Global Perspective*. Malden, MA: Polity, 2013.

———. "Trolling Journalists and the Risks
of Digital Publicity." *Journalism Practice*, advance online publication.
https://doi.org/10.1080/17512786
.2020.1827450.

Watson, Zillah. *VR for News: The New Reality?*
Oxford: Reuters Institute for the
Study of Journalism, 2017.

Weaver, David Hugh, and Lars Willnat. *The
Global Journalist in the 21st Century*.
New York: Routledge, 2012.

Weaver, David Hugh, and Wei Wu. *The
Global Journalist: News People Around
the World*. New York: Hampton
Press, 1998.

Weber, Johannes. "Strassburg, 1605: The Origins of the Newspaper in Europe."
German History 24, no. 3 (2006):
387–412. https://doi.org/10.1191/02663
55406gh3800a.

Weinberger, David. "Transparency Is the
New Objectivity." *Joho the Blog*
(blog), July 19, 2009. http://www
.hyperorg.com/blogger/2009/07/19
/transparency-is-the-new-objectivity.

Welsh, Teresa. "Did the Media Botch the
Boston Bombing?" *US News and
World Report*, April 19, 2013. https://
www.usnews.com/opinion/articles
/2013/04/19/has-media-coverage-of
-boston-marathon-bombings-been
-responsible.

Wenger, Etienne, Richard Arnold McDermott, and William Snyder. *Cultivating
Communities of Practice: A Guide to*

Managing Knowledge. Boston: Harvard Business School Press, 2002.

Wenzel, Andrea, Daniela Gerson, and Evelyn Moreno. "Engaging Communities Through Solutions Journalism." *Tow Center for Digital Journalism*, April 26, 2016. https://www.cjr.org/tow_center _reports/engaging_communities _through_solutions_journalism.php.

Westergaard, Per, and Soren Schultz Jorgensen. "54 Newsrooms, 9 Countries, and 9 Core Ideas: Here's What Two Researchers Found in a Yearlong Quest for Journalism Innovation." *Nieman Lab* (blog), July 11, 2018. https://www.niemanlab.org/2018/07 /54-newsrooms-9-countries-and-9 -core-ideas-heres-what-two -researchers-found-in-a-yearlong -quest-for-journalism-innovation.

Wilhelm, Anthony G. *Democracy in the Digital Age.* New York: Routledge, 2000.

Wilken, Earl. "Behavioral Dynamics Stressed in Front-End Conversion." *Editor and Publisher*, June 14, 1975.

Williams, Raymond. *Television: Technology and Cultural Form.* London: Routledge, 2003.

Witschge, Tamara, and Gunnar Nygren. "Journalistic Work: A Profession Under Pressure?" *Journal of Media Business Studies* 6, no. 1 (2009): 37–59. https://doi.org/10.1080/16522354.2009 .11073478.

Wolfsfeld, Gadi, Elad Segev, and Tamir Sheafer. "Social Media and the Arab Spring: Politics Comes First." *International Journal of Press/Politics* 18, no. 2 (2013): 115–37. https://doi.org/10 .1177/1940161212471716.

Woo, William. "As Old Gods Falter: Public Journalism and the Tradition of Detachment." Presented at the Press-Enterprise Lecture Series, no. 30, University of California, Riverside, February 13, 1995.

Wu, Shangyuan, Edson C. Tandoc, and Charles T. Salmon. "A Field Analysis of Journalism in the Automation Age: Understanding Journalistic Transformations and Struggles Through Structure and Agency." *Digital Journalism* 7, no. 4 (2019): 428–46. https://doi.org/10.1080 /21670811.2019.1620112.

Young, Adreana. "News on the Dash." *Editor and Publisher* 148, no. 6 (June 2015): 8.

Zahra, Shaker A., and Gerard George. "Absorptive Capacity: A Review, Reconceptualization, and Extension." *Academy of Management Review* 27, no. 2 (2002): 185–203. https://doi.org /10.5465/amr.2002.6587995.

Zamith, Rodrigo, Valerie Belair-Gagnon, and Seth C. Lewis. "Constructing Audience Quantification: Social Influences and the Development of Norms About Audience Analytics and Metrics." *New Media and Society* 22, no. 10 (2020): 1763–84. https://doi.org/10.1177 /1461444819881735.

Zelizer, Barbie. "On the Shelf Life of Democracy in Journalism Scholarship." *Journalism* 14, no. 4 (2013): 459–73. https:// doi.org/10.1177/1464884912464179.

———. *Taking Journalism Seriously: News and the Academy.* Thousand Oaks, CA: Sage, 2004.

———. "Why Journalism Is About More Than Digital Technology." *Digital Journalism* 7, no. 3 (2019): 343–50. https://doi.org/10.1080/21670811.2019 .1571932.

Index

140